N... Collins
Adviser, Oxford... Local Education Authority

Oxford University Press

Oxford University Press, Walton Street, Oxford OX2 6DP

Oxford New York Toronto
Delhi Bombay Calcutta Madras Karachi
Petaling Jaya Singapore Hong Kong Tokyo
Nairobi Dar es Salaam Cape Town
Melbourne Auckland

and associated companies in
Beirut Berlin Ibadan Nicosia

Oxford is a trade mark of Oxford University Press

First published 1985
Reprinted 1986, 1987
ISBN 0 19 919067 4

The other cartoons and illustrations are by: Richard Brookes, Anna Hancock and John Hanson.

Typeset by Tradespools Ltd., Frome
Printed in Hong Kong

Introduction

If you have responsibility for the welfare of young people in the classroom, workshop, laboratory, or youth group, this book will help you when you are put on the spot by awkward questions or requests for help. It will also enable you to intervene effectively when young people are experiencing difficulties. It assumes that assessing *what* the problem is, how *urgent* it is, and what is to be *done* are more important to you than speculating about causes or diagnosing specific conditions. It also assumes that you are busy and do not necessarily want to read through pages of sociological or psychiatric theory before you come to the guidelines for action.

This book makes the basic assumption that its readers will be *interested* in young people as individuals, but it does not ignore the fact that you will usually be meeting them in groups. It may be difficult to balance your concern for individuals and the demands of working with groups. In the past there may have been a specialist colleague to whom you could refer individual problems. Such specialists are becoming increasingly rare and there is, in any case, a tide of opinion against such specializations and towards a more integrated and evenly distributed pastoral organization. Of course, young people always went for help to those whom they trusted, regardless of labels, but the chances are that all staff in your establishment are now required to perform pastoral duties. One way or another the pastoral responsibilities of the ordinary teacher, lecturer, or youth trainer have increased.

This is a difficult time to be young, and good support for young people is vital. People may mature earlier now than their parents did, but the transition from adolescence to adulthood is more difficult than ever. Some of the rites of passage such as employment are currently unavailable to many young adults. Rapid social change further confuses the process of transition. But young people are not just transitional organisms, they are worthy of respect and understanding for who and what they are *now*!

In the face of these challenges, *On The Spot* provides two main types of resource: firstly a rapid reference to basic facts and well-tried tactics so that you can help young people deal with particular difficulties; and secondly an indication of the network of professionals who care for young people so that you need not feel isolated and can extend your sense of colleagueship. These resources are offered along with checklists and cautions to help you gauge the seriousness of the situations which confront you and ensure that you are bringing appropriate attention to bear on them.

You may find that there are sections of this book which refer to things with which you are already familiar. There is no assumption about the level of the reader's background knowledge. The text is based on the areas of concern which most frequently cause educators to seek training, information, and guidance. It is also based on the areas in which other professionals, such as health care workers, have uncovered the most uncertainty in their dealings with educators. The result is that if you are just beginning your work with young people you can now be armed in advance with a unique resource book which may save you considerable difficulty. If you are experienced in work with young people you will recognize the key areas of concern and welcome a facility for filling in gaps in your knowledge without having to delve into long reading lists.

It is hoped that this book will become a well-thumbed stand-by. It was enjoyable putting it together and it has been carefully checked by experts in the various fields it covers. I hope you find it useful.

Nigel Collins
Oxford 1984

Note:
In the absence of a better expression, the rather formal and unfriendly word 'client' has been used in this book to refer to the person who is receiving attention and help. It is hoped that this does not undermine the book's primary assumption that a caring and helpful relationship is based on straightforward respect and warmth.

Another linguistic problem is posed by the fact that the use of the masculine pronoun as a general pronoun is misleading. After experiments with such expressions as '(s)he', 'she/he', and 'he (she)', the cumbersome but clear phrase 'he or she' has been used.

Acknowledgements

Among the many people who have helped directly or indirectly with the preparation of the material in this book there are three to whom I am especially grateful:

Dr J.A. Muir Gray is a community health physician, school doctor, and Fellow of Green College, Oxford University. The idea for *On The Spot* came from discussions with him and he supplied much of the impetus for the book. Muir Gray has extensive knowledge of the points of contact between education and health care and has been an invaluable source of guidance and information on this and other projects over a number of years.

Dr Marjory McFarlane recently retired after many years as a Senior Medical Officer with special responsibility for psychosexual counselling and family planning services. In this field Dr McFarlane is a pioneer and I feel privileged to have been able to work with her on various projects including the preparation of parts of this book.

Dr William Ll. Parry-Jones is Consultant Psychiatrist in Administrative Charge of the Highfield Family and Adolescent Unit of the Warneford Hospital, and a Clinical Lecturer in Psychiatry at Oxford University. He is a leading figure in the field of child and adolescent psychiatry and his help with several sections of this book was invaluable. As always working with him was an exciting learning experience and I am deeply grateful for the time he gave, his attention to detail, and his enthusiasm.

Thanks are also due to the following friends:

David Charles-Edwards—Executive Officer for the British Association for Counselling and my personal counsellor for the past seven years.

Stuart Lindeman—TVEI Director (Cumbria LEA) and Training Organizer for the National Association for Young People's Counselling and Advisory Services.

Oliver Howell—Adviser for Community Education (Oxfordshire LEA) and counselling trainer who helped form my ideas on pastoral care.

Sue Bell—Former County Co-ordinator for Health Education (Oxfordshire LEA).

Roger Boulton—Senior Educational Psychologist (Oxfordshire LEA).

Geoff Emerson—Senior Probation Officer and former Intermediate Treatment Officer.

Debbie Green, who typed the manuscript.

My wife Debbie, who put up with all the emotional and behavioural problems which result from trying to produce a book in your spare time and proved the efficacy of several of the techniques described in the book.

Finally, I am grateful for helpful editing and advice from the Education Department of Oxford University Press.

Acknowledgements

Contents

Section A

Some basic ways of offering help

1 Advising

Someone comes to you apparently asking for advice. You have to decide quickly what they actually require. Is it **information** or **suggestions for action**? There is a difference.

Information

Sometimes people simply want the facts (without your evaluation of them or further suggestions for action). If you suspect that this is what is required, and this is a good starting assumption, here are some questions you need to ask yourself:

Do you really understand the request?	To check, try repeating the question in your own words out loud to your client, inviting confirmation that you have got the right end of the stick.
How much information is really required?	A very common fault in most of us is to give too much information—just because we happen to know it. Watch the eyes glaze over.
Do you actually know the answer?	Are you guessing? Are you up-to-date? Have you checked your sources? (It is useful to identify them.)
Are you mixing facts with points of view without differentiating them?	You're allowed points of view and they may be useful, but your client needs to know that's what they are.
Have you checked how much your client knows already?	Don't start from scratch every time. By the time you get to the bit that is needed, your client may have dropped off or given you up.

Making suggestions

We make too many suggestions, especially those of us who work with young people. Have faith in your client's ability to work out a course of action. Given the right information and/or a space in which to think clearly, most people can plan their own actions. In the long run they will be stronger, and their decisions more appropriate, if they arrive at them personally.

Here are some questions you need to ask yourself:

How long has your client got to work things out?	Very occasionally you may be confronted by someone who has to make a very rapid decision and does not have time to work through to a personal plan of action. If you are able to use your personal knowledge and experience to help your client, you may want to make a strong suggestion as to what needs to be done. *But this kind of urgency is extremely rare.*
What are the stakes?	In other words, what happens if your client tries an unsuccessful course of action?
Are you leaving room for your client to reject your suggestions?	You're not going to be hurt if this happens, are you?
If you are issuing imperatives ('must' suggestions), where are the imperatives coming from?—i.e. the law, religious or political principles?	Are you making it clear where they come from? Have you paused long enough to consider whether or not it is actually possible for your client to pursue the course of action you are suggesting?

Some general considerations

1. Can the matter be discussed properly in the present environment?
2. Do you have an axe to grind? Perhaps someone else could offer more dispassionate advice.
3. Are you properly conscious of the ability of your client to understand what you are saying? Are you going over his head or patronizing her?
4. Conversely, are you allowing prejudice, whether racial, sexual, or classist to colour your advice?

5 Have you worked out what you are going to do about confidentiality? Make your decision clear.

6 Does your client really need counselling? Don't keep referring to the issue every time you see your client. Make it clear whether or not the person can get further help from you and then leave them to seek it as far as possible. *People need to be able to move on and leave difficulties behind.*

7 It's worth checking out why you have been approached in the first place. Are there other people your client trusts enough to ask for help? If not, you will be helping if you enable them to find others they trust. Don't revel in being 'the only person I can really talk to about this'.

8 Use appropriate leaflets etc., but not as a substitute for person-to-person discussion.

9 Make judicious use of referral if you feel out of your depth.

10 Your experience and knowledge as an adult may be useful, but don't embellish the facts. Also remember that you have not lived the same life as your client and therefore, although you may think that you've 'been through this' yourself, there will be differences. Recounting the details of your own personal triumphs in adversity may impress *you* more than help the person to whom you are responding.

11 Don't get too caught up in the drama of your client's problem. What is normally useful for someone at a crossroads is a good solid signpost with clearly marked information, not a cloaked figure waving a banner and swearing to get you through at all costs.

2 Counselling

Counselling is a situation in which a person attempts to explore and clarify ways of improving his or her situation by expressing feelings and thoughts connected with that situation to another person who has set aside the time to help this process. The person who seeks help is usually referred to as the 'client'. The person who offers the help is the 'counsellor'. There are many styles of counselling but most counsellors agree that a counselling situation has the following features:

1. It is a relationship based on mutual respect.
2. It is voluntary on the part of the client.
3. The counsellor is 'for' the client in that at the time of the counselling session he or she has no other business but helping the client.
4. The counsellor intrudes and interrupts only to help the client to clarify his or her feelings and thoughts.
5. The counsellor is non-critical of the client or any information which the client chooses to disclose.
6. The client is only in the role of client during the time agreed for the counselling to take place.

The counselling situation

A person indicates that he or she is upset. At this stage you do not know what the problem is. Here are some simple procedures which should enable you to be helpful.

Ask yourself:

1. Is this person actually seeking help?

   NO Consider leaving the matter alone. Weigh up whether this person knows how to ask for help. If not, you may decide to proceed as if help had been solicited.

   YES Proceed to the next question.

2. Is the help asked for specific?

   YES Supply it. We all know that people hide deep problems behind trivial ones, but in the style of counselling suggested here *the simple always precedes the complex*.

   NO Make it clear that you are prepared to give attention. Give free attention.

Free attention

This consists simply of listening calmly and intently, looking at the other person in a sympathetic but not sentimental way. Above all it means listening rather than talking. Talk only to help when your client gets stuck and to give reassurance that you are still paying attention. The object is to draw the person's difficulties out into the open where they can be examined.

Checklist

1 Are you doing the talking? *Don't: listen.*

2 Are you being critical, either by speech or by expression? Don't at this stage. You need to be very sure that you know what the problem is and that your opinion is useful before expressing it.

3 Are you colluding? In other words are you agreeing with emotional statements like 'I hate X...' or 'I'm so frightened of doing Y...'? Don't collude. This is not your session. It is not helpful to switch the focus from the other person's feelings to your own.

4 Are you letting what is being said upset you? Don't. This is not about *your* feelings. If you can't keep away from your own feelings long enough to give good attention, you should admit this and help find someone who can.

5 Are you making it obvious that you respect your client and that you are going to remain calm, caring, and unshockable?
If it is true, do so. If it is not true, do not pretend to be helping.

Going deeper

Very often free attention is all that is needed for a person to identify what is bothering them, share the feeling, and move towards a solution or a position of greater strength. Sometimes, however, things are not so simple and more work and more help are needed.

If you have tried giving free attention and it has become apparent that more active help is needed, you need to ask yourself:

1 Am I in a position to give more help to this person?

2 Do I have the time?

3 Will I uncover information about this person which will make life impossible for one or both of us?

If you decide that you *can* give further help this is the time to remind yourself of the object of the exercise.

The object of counselling is to enable a person who is your equal to find the strength within him or herself to overcome a difficulty using his or her own strategy. There is no person who does not have the strength to do this.

Checklist

1 Are you trying to be clever, or are you looking for simple approaches which will help the person you are counselling?

2 Are you encouraging the natural forms of release of tension and confusion—crying, shaking, raging, laughing? You do need to protect people from ridicule, however.

3 Don't go off at tangents. This may be a way of avoiding important issues which are painful to deal with but must sooner or later be faced. Why not now?

4 If your client 'dries up', don't be afraid to ask for repetition of ground already covered.

5 Try to keep your client talking in the 'I' form. It keeps people nearer the feelings they have got to deal with.

6 Give your client reassurance that he or she is strong enough to face up to whatever is upsetting them, however awful it may seem.

7 Don't allow total negativity to set in. Get your client to rephrase things in a more positive way.

8 Many people forget that we all have problems and they feel bad about asking for counselling. Be sure to say to all people you counsel things you like about them and express admiration for things they have achieved. If you can't think of any you are either not trying hard enough or you shouldn't be counselling this person.

9 Counselling is important and working through one's difficulties is sometimes painful—*but don't let the session get too grim.*

10 Get your client to clarify his or her own muddles. Go back over ground until things are beginning to become clear. But remember—this is not for your benefit. The fact that you don't understand may not be important. You are aiming to enable your client to see the situation clearly.

Endings

Your long-term aim may be to help someone overcome a deep-seated difficulty, but between sessions life must go on. Endings are, therefore, very important.

Your aim at the end of a session is to get the other person into a fit frame of mind to cope with immediate responsibilities with as much dignity and strength as possible.

Checklist

1 Be clear about the timing of the session and indicate when there are about five minutes left.

2 Get your client's attention away from the area you have been exploring with him or her and back on to the immediate environment. Make your client look around and describe things that are in the room and talk about the things he or she will shortly be doing.

3 *Always end on a positive note.* Find a compliment about the way your client has worked in the session. Ask for a very brief description of a recent enjoyable or satisfying accomplishment. Ask for something that your client is looking forward to doing.

4 Be clear about whether or not you are going to be available for further counselling and arrange details now if possible.

5 Reaffirm confidentiality.

General

1 Always be clear about confidentiality from the beginning. Check without delay that the limits of your confidentiality (if any) are understood.

2 Don't let your client become too dependent on you. If you see this developing, find ways of helping him or her to stand alone or use others (especially peers) for support.

3 Try to strike a balance between passing the buck and pretending to be more competent than you really are. You may need to refer your client to someone else. See the next section on referral.

Questions for would-be counsellors

1 Are *you* the problem?

2 Are you working on your own problems? We all have problems. We can all find counsellors.

3 Do you need more training in counselling? There is a reading list at the back of this book but it is no substitute for practical guidance. There are organizations in most areas which run counselling courses. You may be surprised at the way such courses develop your confidence and understanding as well as increasing your skill and knowledge.

3 Referral

One meaning of the verb 'to refer' is 'to hand over a question to some special or ultimate authority for consideration, decision, execution, etc.' Young people are frequently referred from one person to another and most professionals both give and receive many referrals in the course of a year. The ideal model of referral is one in which professional A hands over a problem at the point at which he or she has reached the limits of his or her competence to professional B, whom he or she believes to be more competent.

Referrals are not only made to tap new skills, in the hope of relieving the young person. They are also made to relieve the professional. Referrals may be made to shift the responsibility to another's desk—'just to cover ourselves: I think we'd better refer'; or to share anxiety—'I'm not sure what to do next; I think I'll refer.'

Often all these motives are present and if they are it is important they be recognized. There is nothing reprehensible in referring a person's problem because you are anxious or wish to transfer the responsibility, but it can be confusing to the professional to whom it is referred if he or she does not appreciate your motives. The reason such motives are not always notified is that the referrer is not always aware of them.

Before making a referral, therefore, ask yourself:

1. Why am I referring this problem? Is it:
   a for expert advice?
   b to shift some of the responsibility?
   c to share my anxiety?
2. Why am I referring the person now and not yesterday or last week?
3. Have I chosen the most appropriate referral point?
4. What does my client think about the referral?
5. Have I made all these points clear in my referral letter?

When receiving a referral

It is often flattering to receive a referral, but before focusing on the problem referred it is often helpful to ask a few questions about the referral itself.

Ask the referrer:

1. 'What is the principal problem?'
   (If the answer is 'everything', ask for the three most difficult problems.)
2. 'Tell me what you have tried so far.'
3. 'How were you hoping that I would be able to help?'
   (A more acceptable way of asking the key question, 'What do you expect me to do?')
4. 'Can you write me a note covering these points please?' Sometimes 'the problem' disappears when the referrer tries to write it down; often the act of writing distils and clarifies the referrer's difficulties with the problem.

4 Dealing with risk

Young people often indicate to us directly or indirectly that they are taking, or being subjected to risks. We want to protect them from injury or other catastrophes so we tend to issue warnings. Nine times out of ten they don't work. Here are some suggestions for avoiding doomed approaches to helping young people deal with risk.

Approaches to avoid

1. Don't refer to the seriousness of the risk or the dangers involved. To many young people, danger is an incentive. Unlike you, they may not review their lives in relation to dependents or responsibilities. They seek excitement and they associate it with danger. Accidents and 'serious' illness may be

associated in the minds of teenagers with days off school and extra sympathy and attention. In the same context, advice centring on safety will make little impact because safety is seen as boring and a rejection of the excitement to be had from danger.

2 Don't waste your breath warning people about possible death in middle age—an approach frequently used to combat smoking. Young people cannot easily imagine being old and may have little desire for longevity. They associate old age with decrepitude. They probably don't even want to be middle-aged since they are not impressed by the examples of it which they see around them. Some of them think old age starts at about 25 anyway.

3 Reference to long-term dangers or long-term benefits are useless. Young people do not often see far ahead in their lives. They are struggling to cope with the challenges of their rapidly changing sense of identity and role. They want immediate returns for immediate efforts.

4 Don't goad young people to reject bad influences. You are asking them to relinquish a sense of normality, belonging, being wanted, and identity. This cannot be tackled head-on.

5 In general an authoritarian approach is counter-productive. Adolescence and young adulthood are times when the person has to challenge existing beliefs and attitudes is order to formulate a personal ethic. By giving directives, however benevolent, you are merely offering an opportunity for rejection.

Positive approaches

1 Give information dispassionately where it is known. Don't use emotive words like 'danger'.

2 Stress competence rather than safety. Young people respond to the challenge of acquiring new skills. For example, many would rather see themselves as skilful riders than as safe ones.

3 If you want to bring home the consequences of risks, refer to disability rather than death. Not many people of any age can consider death and our social system tidies death away from us. However, there are daily reminders of disability.

4 Stress *short-term* benefits wherever possible in counselling about health risks. They may seem to you to be less significant than the long-term benefits (e.g. looking good and not smelling of tobacco versus avoiding lung cancer and heart disease) but your client may take the opposite view.

5 Help young people to understand how peer group pressure works. Try to tackle whole groups without isolating people. Assertiveness training to resist peer pressures can be of great benefit to individuals but is not easy to undertake.

6 Get alongside your client rather than issuing warnings from a great height. After all, you take risks too, don't you?

7 Encourage debate on social and personal issues. Risk-taking is related to personal values. People have to thrash out a priority list for their lives. It won't be the same as yours.
There is no life without risk. We are forced to gamble all the time. Your job is to see that the young people are playing with the fullest deck available, and that they know the stakes, before they place their bets.

Section B

Dealing with particular problem areas

1 The development of young people

Physical development of young people

The period of adolescence is characterized by an acceleration in the rate of physical growth linked to sexual maturation. Although people grow rapidly throughout their childhood, adolescence is the particular phase during which this growth rate is fastest.

The reason for this acceleration is that the hormonal balance of the young person changes. There is an increase in anabolic steroids, the hormones which have received much publicity in recent years for the impact they have on the size and performance of those athletes who take them in synthetic form.

Increased size and strength in adolescence are linked to sexual maturity and another effect of the hormonal changes is to make the young person fertile. The point at which the person becomes fertile is usually known as puberty. In girls puberty is dramatically marked by their first period, known as the menarche. In boys the transition is not so dramatic but there is a gradual increase in sperm count during the early stage of adolescence. The hormones responsible for these developments are the oestrogens (in females) and androgens (in males).

As with any other biological feature, the time at which adolescence begins and ends varies from person to person. In general, girls have their adolescence earlier than boys; but this varies a great deal both amongst girls, and amongst boys, so that some boys begin their adolescence before some girls do.

There is much concern about both precocious and delayed puberty but such cases are in fact extremely rare. Most of the cases where a young person, his or her relatives, or the GP think that puberty is precocious or delayed are in fact examples of young people at one extreme or the other of the normal range. It is, however, very important to remember that fears about delayed puberty are very common among young people and that the young person may need confirmation that he or she is 'normal' when the signs of sexual development do not appear as early as they have done in friends.

For boys the general practitioner should be a useful source of support but for girls the general practitioner may not be appropriate if the practitioner is a man. In such cases it may be more appropriate to seek the advice of the health visitor or the school nurse.

Social influences on physical development

The variation in development that can be observed when looking at a group of young people is principally due to genetic factors. A young person inherits a number of genes affecting the timing and rate of his or her sexual development and the age of puberty. Social factors are also important and the best evidence for this is that as the health and nutritional condition of children has improved, so the age of puberty has declined. This is clearly illustrated if the age of female puberty in a number of different European countries is studied in relation to its decline throughout this century. There is, however, some evidence that this trend may be coming to an end and that in some countries, and in some social classes, young girls have now reached the biological limits of puberty. Further improvements in health and nutrition are unlikely to lead to a further decline in the age of the menarche.

Because the age of puberty is not so clear-cut in boys as in girls, there is no comparable data for young men. However, as the height and weight of young men has increased steadily during this century, and as the prevalence of malnutrition has decreased, it is reasonable to suppose that the age of puberty has declined in males too.

Chronological age and developmental age

Chronological age is the age of an individual in years; developmental age is the age at which particular characteristics are usually found. For example, someone whose adolescence begins early will have a developmental age that is older than his or her chronological age and someone whose adolescence begins late will have a developmental age that is younger than his or her chronological age.

The rate at which various stages in development become evident varies from one person to another but there is a general sequence of events and this sequence is co-ordinated. As a result of this it is important to consider that young people whose sexual development is more advanced will also have other body systems that are more advanced. This may affect learning and athletic capabilities. Attempts have been made to group young people by developmental age for education and sport, but the complexities of this are considerable and it is therefore customary for chronological age, the age in years, to be used as the means of grouping young people. It has been noted that if young people look mature they tend to be treated more like adults and that this has an affect on their progress. The converse, in late developers, has also been noted and gives cause for some concern.

Emotional development in adolescence

At the same time as coming to terms with physical growth and sexual development, each adolescent has to learn to separate from his or her own family and build satisfactory relationships outside it. This process of separation takes time and does not proceed at a steady rate. Young people may take opportunities to reach towards adult independence but they also have moments when they appear to revert to childlike dependence. Their lives are often full of tensions between these two impulses.

Quite obviously some young people have more supportive social circumstances than others. Some are getting clear messages about what sort of behaviour is expected of them and are being tolerated as they reconcile this with new and powerful feelings. The lucky ones have a semi-safe environment in which to experiment. It has to be semi-safe because it must not be so protective that it shields them entirely from the consequences of their actions. Other young people are getting confused messages about what is expected of them and are being punished for their experiments with social behaviour. If the confusion or conflict is too extreme, emotional development may be retarded or become distorted. Disturbed behaviour will result.

In order to mature, people need to interact. Much learning will take place in the peer group but it is also helpful for young people to be able to relate to people older than themselves. For some their school, college, or youth group may provide useful contact with experienced adults and a semi-safe environment in which to mature. For others the framework of the institution and the roles of the adults within it will only add to their confusion. The most common area of confusion caused, or worsened, by uncaring institutions is over what constitutes 'normal' behaviour.

Young people are deeply concerned about normality and prone to anxiety about the possibility that they are 'abnormal'. There is actually a very wide range of 'normal' feelings and behaviours and this fact should be relayed to young people. There is a difference however between what is 'normal' in the sense of being quite common and unharmful, and what is 'normal' in the sense of being accepted by a particular institution. If an institution does not make this difference plain it will seriously undermine the emotional development of young people. A classic example is the way in which institutions punish the expression of quite natural (and mainly transient) homosexual feelings.

One of the problems facing caring institutions which group their members according to age or specific abilities is that there is no common timetable for emotional development. In any school year group or academic set there will be people at quite different stages of development—or to put it more accurately, people developing quite different aspects of their personalities. This problem is made more complex by the fact that physical development gives misleading clues about emotional development. Educators are therefore faced with the task of giving appropriate support and guidance to people whose appearance may give a wrong impression of their emotional maturity.

One of the characteristics of emotional development in adolescence is the questioning of parental values. This may be accompanied by a complete verbal rejection of parents or a denial that parents are of any significance in the young person's life. The truth of the matter is that young people are more emotionally involved with their parents (or guardians) than they are with their peers or other adults, however vigorously they may deny this. They will have absorbed more of their parents' values than even the parents may have realized.

In our society, inadequate training is given for the important job of parenting and many parents do not understand how to adapt to take account of the transition of their children into adulthood. The result is that the emotional development of young people often has to proceed with haphazard or inappropriate support and guidance from parents. It does not help that the extended family, although it is still important, is geographically dispersed. Communication is largely via the telephone and the direct personal contact with grandparents or aunts and uncles may not be as available as it once was. Young people may therefore be exposed to fewer alternative models of parenting and may rely more and more heavily on teachers and youth workers for reassurance when their own parents are causing them anxiety.

The most conducive environment for emotional development in adolescence would be one in which young people were made to feel important as individuals; given clear feedback about their behaviour; given scope to experiment with relationships (and the expression of their feelings) within clear but tolerant boundaries; and presented with consistent and caring models of adult behaviour. In such an environment young people would never hear in a sarcastic or angry voice the mysterious order—'Grow up!'

Social development of young people

The word 'adolescence' has no precise meaning in relation to social development. There is no legal definition and no other social instrument attempts to define it. Doctors and psychologists would expect adolescence to begin within the age range 11–14 and it is possible to describe certain life tasks which become important at the same time. These are listed below. On the other hand there is no possibility of stating when these tasks are likely to be completed; indeed, many are incapable of completion. In social terms, when does an adolescent become an adult? Our society has never been able to decide.

The truth is that the main social concerns of young people are the same as the main social concerns of adults. The difference is that young people are meeting these concerns consciously for the first time and are preoccupied with developing the skills and perspectives required to deal with them. These life-long social concerns centre around the following:

a Establishing and constantly reviewing social identity (**roles**).
b Understanding and adjusting to other people (**relationships**).
c Developing and constantly reviewing a personal code of behaviour (**morals**).
d Developing and maintaining a degree of independence (**autonomy**).
e Discovering ways of contributing to, and benefiting from, life in society (**community**).

What is mistaken for pointless rebellion is often part of the quest for skills in the above areas. Listening to the opinions and experiences of other people does not give a person new skills, although it may help to form perspectives. Young people need to challenge received wisdom in order to discover if it is sound—all too often it is not. They need to experiment with ways of doing things in case the old ways are not the best—how else is society to progress?

There is so much focus on the provocative aspects of young people's behaviour that their great urge to conform is often missed. They challenge in order to discover the true foundations of conformity. The vast majority want to be accepted: not patronized or tolerated, but respected. Even if things go badly wrong and individual young people become alienated from society, they seek out sub-cultures, many of which have very demanding and inflexible norms, in order to be accepted somewhere. Indeed much unhappiness in young people is made worse by their reluctance to approach adults who might be able to help them, in case the helpers find something seriously wrong with them.

Most educators realize that although they are only a part of the field of influence on the social development of young people, they are an important part. The skills, attitudes, and values of educators are under review the whole time, and hypocrisy and inconsistency will not be missed. The best helpers of young people are those who have a balanced view of their own social development. Such people know that they can offer guidance, and some models for behaviour, but they accept that they are still developing themselves and have much to learn. They feel a rapport with young people in their attempts to discover what matters and whether things can be tackled better by the new generation of adults than they were by the old.

2 Physical health problems

Disease and illness in adolescence

Disease

It is very important to distinguish between disease and illness in adolescence. A disease may be defined as anything that doctors wish to call a disease. You may think this is a tautology since diseases seem to be self-evident entities (e.g. tuberculosis or asthma). It is, however, important to remember that doctors change their minds about what constitutes a disease from time to time and drop some diseases from the classification of diseases while adding others to it. For example, many young people in times past were made to lead a quiet and sheltered life because it was thought that they had a disease called 'disorderly action of the heart'. It is now known that the heart murmur that was considered to be diagnostic of this disease is not an indication of disease but is the normal heart sound in a healthy adolescent. This disease has therefore been dropped from the classification. Similarly, other diseases have been added to the classification and in recent years we have seen the addition of anorexia nervosa and bulimia to the list of diseases that occur in adolescence. Undoubtedly these diseases occurred in times past but were not recognized as diseases.

Illness

An illness is not a pathological condition: it is a social condition. The person who is ill obtains certain rewards, notably increased sympathy and being excused from normal obligations like going to school or going to work. For a person to obtain the rewards of illness, however, he or she has to satisfy colleagues, friends and family that he or she is 'really ill' by following certain rules. He or she should appear ill; should seek help if the illness does not clear up within 24 or 48 hours; should try to get better, for example by following the advice given by a doctor or nurse; and should give up some normal social pleasures during the period in which he or she expects to receive the privileges of being ill. We are all in the business of either seeking or validating illness all the time and in most cases we do it well. In some cases, however, the doctor is called in to decide whether or not someone is 'really ill'.

If the doctor finds that the person who is frequently off school, or claims to be too tired to help with the housework, has a disease, then it is accepted that the person is 'really ill'. Often, however, it is not possible for the doctor to identify any definite disease affecting the person who claims to be ill. This throws suspicion on the person's claim but does not invalidate it completely. If, for example, a young person says that he or she has recurrent headaches, the doctor cannot say that the person does not have headaches. The doctor can say that it is unlikely that the young person has migraine, if the headaches do not fall into the classical pattern of migraine, but he or she cannot deny a young person's claim to be suffering from pains in the head.

Illness is a political act. It can shift the balance of power within the family or within an institution. It allows the young person to be excused from doing homework or seeking work. It is not surprising therefore that young people, and those they encounter, are frequently involved in debates about whether or not someone is 'really ill'.

Disease and illness

The person who has a disease can claim the status of being ill. In acute diseases such as influenza the onset of illness is obvious because the young person is physically incapacitated. Recovery is often more gradual than onset, and it may be difficult to decide between a person being 'well enough' to go back to work or school or continuing to be so ill that it is justifiable for him or her to stay at home.

The decision a young person makes to relinquish the privileges of illness and return to normal social duties, whether school, work, or family life, is complex, and is influenced by many factors.

Some young people with a chronic disease, however, take a completely opposite approach to the management of the social consequences of disease. They do everything in their power to avoid being ill. They do not seek sympathy or ask to be excused from normal social duties, and even though they feel unwell from time to time they go out of their way to ignore the rules of illness and the privileges of being ill. The young person with diabetes, for example, will usually try to lead a 'normal life'. The position can be complicated by parental anxiety. Parents of a youngster diagnosed as having asthma or diabetes may become so anxious that even though they believe they are trying to help the youngster lead 'a normal life', they are surrounding him or her with subtle pressures that make life difficult and make the young person ill no matter how strong the wish to be normal.

Common physical health problems

Adolescence in the UK is now a healthy time of life, at least from the physical perspective. Fifty or sixty years ago adolescents suffered many chronic diseases such as tuberculosis, osteomyelitis, and rheumatic fever. These diseases are now uncommon and chronic disabling disease is now rare in adolescence.

If a youngster has a severe chronic disability such as diabetes or asthma he or she will usually know a great deal about it and will not need any technical advice on how best to manage the condition. He or she may, however, need help with social adjustment. Usually some simple questions such as:

'What's it like having diabetes? Does it make any difference to your life?'

'Do your parents worry about it much?'

will reveal underlying anxieties if the young person has a good relationship with the questioner. The problem rarely lies with the young person; it usually lies with the parent. On the other hand, young people often have vague and ill-defined symptoms of which headaches and tiredness are the most common.

Tiredness

It is commonly thought that tiredness is a symptom of anaemia, especially in girls; but in fact tiredness is very rarely caused by anaemia. Anaemia—low levels of haemoglobin in the blood—is itself very uncommon in adolescence. It hardly ever occurs in boys and when it occurs in girls it is normally the result of very heavy menstrual bleeding. Some adolescents who follow a very strict vegan diet may also become anaemic.

Boredom may produce signs which are similar to those of tiredness, but in most cases tiredness has a simple cause: insufficient sleep or too much physical exertion.

Paleness

Parents are often worried that adolescent children look pale. They may express this as a fear that the youngster is physically unwell, but this anxiety often hides the true anxiety, namely that the youngster is leading a life of debauchery or is 'on drugs'. Again, drugs are an uncommon cause of paleness. Some people are naturally paler than others and some young people just do not spend much time in the fresh air or sun.

As with tiredness, young people who are the cause of severe anxiety for their parents should be encouraged to go and see their general practitioner because a blood test will almost always exclude anaemia.

Headaches

Headaches are common in adolescence and are also a source of great concern to parents and teachers. Very very rarely are headaches due to anything serious such as a brain tumour.

Headaches which are a symptom of migraine usually follow a classical pattern. They occur on one side of the head; they may be accompanied by vomiting; and the young person may feel unwell before the headache starts. Headaches which are not due to migraine may be what is usually called 'tension headaches', or alcoholic hangovers; in either case the best remedy is a common painkiller such as Disprin.

Obesity (fatness)

Many people worry about their weight and shape. The current fashion for slimness makes matters worse. The number of people who have a physical health problem from obesity is far fewer than the number who have an emotional problem related to dissatisfaction with the amount of fat they are carrying. The social problem of being teased about being overweight can be very distressing for young people.

There is now considerable evidence that obesity increases the likelihood of certain heart conditions which don't usually manifest themselves before people are in their thirties. It is therefore essential that young people have information and guidance about diet and exercise. It is also important that they can rely on good counselling if they are worried about the way they look. Don't forget that there is a wide range of normal healthy body shapes.

If you concentrate your attention on helping the person to establish a positive self-image and developing an intelligent approach to diet and exercise, you are likely to be useful. If the person is not accepted by peers because of appearance, you may have to work with the group to change attitudes and foster peer group support. If in doubt about obesity, ask the school nurse or health visitor for advice.

General malaise

Many young people go through periods when they are not sure whether they are tired, ill, bored, depressed, or just muddled. Usually these periods are short and the person is able to sort out his or her own problems. Counselling will often expedite this sorting out and may be able to help someone deal with lingering confusion about his or her state of health.

3 Emotional and behavioural problems

Assessing the seriousness of the problem

People may behave in a very odd fashion or become very distressed and still require quite straightforward help. The suggested approach to counselling at the beginning of this book will enable you to be of use to people with a variety of problems. A very small number of people are likely to be suffering from a disorder which requires psychiatric help. It is not your responsibility to go looking for such people. Neither is it helpful for you to try to attach diagnostic labels to various forms of disorders. On the other hand, you may become sufficiently worried about someone to feel that you need to make some form of assessment of the severity of their problems. This is not an easy task, but if you approach it in a systematic way, relying particularly on your own observation of the person's behaviour, the severity of the situation will usually become quite clear. You will then be in a good position, if necessary, to supply useful information to any specialist who is called in to help.

If you are very worried about someone, what you will be trying to assess is the severity of their emotional or behavioural disorder. The following is a framework which may help you to do so.

Start by concentrating on behaviour using your own observations. What is it that your client is doing or saying that worries you? Presumably it is worrying because it is inconsistent with how you would expect him or her to behave. Is it inconsistent with his or her

- age?
- sex?
- intelligence?
- social background?
- usual disposition or character?

In addition you need to establish how far-reaching the odd behaviour is. This will involve such considerations as:

1 *Where* does the client behave in a worrying fashion?
Is it any one place or everywhere he or she goes?

2 Is there a particular *circumstance* which provokes the odd behaviour?

3 Is he or she behaving oddly with *particular people* or with everyone?

4 *How long* has he or she been behaving like this?

5 Have you observed any *change or development* in the behaviour? Is it getting more puzzling or alarming or is it fairly constant?

Having pinned down the nature of the worrying behaviour you will be in a position to gauge the seriousness of the situation. There are a number of more difficult questions which you might ask yourself about your client. They are difficult because you are progressing from strict observation to gauging the person's emotional state, and the effect he or she will have on others.

1 Is your client suffering? If so, is there any reason to believe that the suffering will continue indefinitely without intervention?

2 Is your client causing, or likely to cause, suffering to others?

3 Is there a possibility that your client's behaviour will alienate him or her from society, friends, family peer group, etc.?

4 Is the way your client is behaving likely to affect adversely his or her educational attainment?

5 Is your client likely to attempt suicide?

6 Do you think your client knows what is going on in the environment? Is there anything that appears to suggest that he or she has a distorted view of reality?

Remembering that your starting point is tangible evidence, if you find that you are answering 'yes' to the above questions you should seek assistance. If you are a school teacher, your school should have a referral system which you can bring into use. In colleges and youth groups such referral systems do not always exist and you may have to discuss with colleagues how best to arrange referral to a psychiatrist (see sections on referral, p. 14, and child psychiatrists, p. 96).

The chances are, however, that you will decide that the situation is not sufficiently serious to warrant referral. Young people seldom require psychiatric help. Please note also that it is not suggested that you make a habit of closely observing the behaviour of young people and trying to assess their emotional state. These are only guidelines to use for cases which cause you particular concern.

Anxiety

What is it?

It is helpful to regard the term 'anxiety' as referring to a continuum of conditions with worry at one extreme and identifiable psychiatric disorders, such as phobic anxiety, at the other. Between the extremes is a range of conditions which may or may not require psychiatric attention.

When human beings are faced with threat, danger, or challenge, they normally go into a state of readiness for action which one might call 'alarm'. In this state, the body prepares for physical effort, the senses are sharpened, and the speed of thinking is increased. This instinctive reaction has obvious survival value. It enables us to overcome adversity. Sometimes the reaction is triggered by situations in which we are not actually able to respond physically or mentally to the challenge because it is beyond our power to do so. In this case, the state of alarm, of readiness, is a nuisance because it upsets us for no good purpose. The extra energy released ready for emergency action is liable to have to be burned off through purposeless behaviour and we may feel tense and distressed without knowing what to do about it. In our society we are continually being triggered into a state of alarm without being able to act. We use the term *anxiety* to describe the apprehensiveness which results. This happens to all of us to some degree and the first thing one can say about anxiety is that there is no point in telling people they shouldn't feel it. Why add an extra burden to their problems?

Anxiety, then, is a prolonged state of alarm or apprehension. It has certain physical aspects such as muscular tension, which may be visible as facial tension, awkward body posture, fidgeting, and meaningless or exaggerated gestures. It also has emotional aspects such as irritability and impatience. Intellectually it impairs concentration.

So far we have been talking about a type of anxiety which is very common, which comes and goes and responds well to ordinary counselling. At the other end of the continuum are anxiety states which will be beyond your help unless you are a therapist. These conditions are not necessarily attributable to environmental factors and they can affect the life of the sufferer. Such psychiatric anxiety disorders are not common and the majority of people you counsel will not need therapy.

It is possible for people to be habitually slightly anxious without suffering from a disorder which needs therapy. To describe people who are prone to mild states of ongoing anxiety we talk about 'worriers' and 'nervous types'. If you look carefully at the section on assessing the seriousness of emotional problems (pp. 26–7) you will have a framework for estimating whether you are dealing with a worrier or someone needing psychiatric help.

Psychiatrists take different standpoints about the causes of anxiety states which do not seem to be reactions to specific situations. Freudians argue that such anxiety arises from deep-seated conflicts which are part of the human condition. The harder a person tries to keep them out of their conscious thoughts, the more devastating their effect will be if they ever do surface. Thus the strong-willed fall hardest in the end. Behaviourists argue that such anxiety is learned as a response to certain 'no-win' experiences such as:

—situations where your sense of worth or identity is seriously undermined;
—circumstances which constantly remind you of extremely unpleasant personal experiences;
—situations which diminish your sense of personal power to direct your life;
—situations in which the immediate future is so unpredictable that you can never prepare yourself in advance for the impact of the next event;
—certain illnesses, impairments, and physical upheavals.

Young people are particularly prone to anxiety and so are the middle-aged. Both groups face a major adjustment to new physical and emotional changes. Young people, however, have a limited perspective on life and their fears are liable to get out of proportion, making anxiety more acute. The expression of anxiety is also more noticeable among young people, who may not have developed social tactics for disguising their feelings; it is unwise to assess the seriousness of anxiety in young people in relation to norms of adult behaviour.

Anxiety states can take many forms. One common form is anxious self-concern in which people become obsessed with their own well-being. In extreme cases this may mean that the person is convinced that he or she has a disease or mental illness and actually exhibits some of the symptoms. Because of the rapid and important physical changes associated with adolescence, young people frequently go through a period of anxious self-concern.

Educators need to be sensitive to the concern young people feel about the way they look, new physical feelings, and the evidence of major changes in the ways their bodies work. Some aspects of school or youth group routine, such as compulsory communal showers, may add considerably to the distress youngsters are already feeling. As the rate of change slows and their bodies become more settled, most young adults worry less about their shape and state of health.

Another common form of anxiety is phobic anxiety. Phobias are irrational fears which are out of all proportion to the situation. Some phobias are specific to a single situation; it might be a type of environment, an object, an animal, or a social situation. Others are more general and may develop cumulatively. In extreme cases people suffering from phobic anxiety may go through elaborate precautionary rituals to avoid encountering the thing that is feared—even if there is only a remote chance of such an encounter. At this extreme phobic anxiety can be seriously disabling.

The phobias you are most likely to encounter in young people are those which involve a fear of some social or environmental situation. Social phobias may disappear as the individual matures and is forced by exposure to become less sensitive to the situations which are feared. Very occasionally they will persist and only therapy will help.

What can you do?

Various suggestions about helping distressed people have already been made in the section on counselling. Here are some more suggestions related specifically to anxiety.

1 *Learn from your own anxiety* Examine your experience of anxiety. Distinguish specific worries from the general feelings of anxiety. How do you deal with them? If you manage to avoid general feelings of anxiety, give some thought to how this is achieved.

2 *Be reassuring about 'normality'* A common cause of anxiety among young people is their doubt about being normal. Don't allow talk about abnormality to get out of hand. Try to show young people what a wide range of so-called normality exists. Don't let people use loaded words like 'deviant' or 'abnormal' without asking for explanations. Don't use them yourself at all. Even if you are presented with accounts of quite extraordinary behaviour, react calmly and find out as much as you can, rather than making judgements.

3 *Instil a sense of personal power* Be optimistic about the ability of the anxious person to cope with or overcome difficulties and feelings. Encourage the person to recall occasions when he or she overcame adversity. Tap into that personal power which the anxiety is obscuring. Get a perspective on troubled times by drawing out the good things that are happening and the strong points in the person's personality. The basic message is 'you may feel anxious but you are not defeated'.

4 *Reframing* A useful weapon in combating anxiety is known as 'reframing'. It means describing a feeling or a situation in a different (usually more positive) way. It is not just a game with words but an effective way of helping someone to change an attitude.

For example a person may say to you:

'Everything I do makes my parents unhappy.'

That may be how it feels, but what is the evidence? A reframing might be:

'X, Y and Z make my parents unhappy but my parents appreciate the way I do A, B, and C.'

Generalizations which indicate helplessness can be reframed so that a person's power and skills are mentioned.

'Once you've been in court nobody trusts you so you might as well steal.'

This is an understandable but unhelpful feeling which needs to be reframed along the lines of:

'If you've been in court you have to work harder to convince some people that you can be trusted. I can do that because I'm a very determined person.'

Some statements about a situation which are couched in completely negative terms can be reframed to throw entirely new light on the situations:

'I can't see any girl ever wanting to have anything to do with me. I'm not hard enough. I can't help it but I just cry when I get unhappy. Girls don't go for weak men.'

A possible reframing would be along the lines:

'I'm lucky really because I feel things quite deeply and I know how to get unhappiness out of my system. There must be plenty of girls who prefer a boyfriend who is sensitive.'

If someone simply cannot make positive statements about their situation, try getting them to exaggerate how bad it is. Even do it for them, but lightly, not aggressively. With any luck the absurdity will cause laughter. Spontaneous mirth is a sign that something is being seen in perspective. That is exactly what you are after.

Depression

What is it?

It is useful to regard the term 'depression' as referring to a continuum of conditions at one end of which are states of despondency and dejection which are readily understandable, and at the other depressive illness. Like everyone else, young people may suffer from lowering of mood for short periods of time. In most cases the occurrence of sadness or despondency will be no more striking than periods of calm or exhilaration. Occasionally, however, you will notice, or be approached by, young people who seem unable to shake off feelings of dejection. The fact that someone is having difficulty dealing with a low mood does not necessarily mean they are suffering from a depressive illness. Such illnesses are relatively rare, especially among young people. What actually differentiates the two ends of the continuum is the degree to which the depression is related to internal or external factors. There are depressive illnesses which are almost totally unrelated to the person's life situation. Rather, they are probably related to internal psychological processes or biochemical changes.

The majority of people who receive medical treatment for depression fall into the middle areas of the continuum where external factors, such as bereavement, may be associated with intrinsic factors which have predisposed the person to depression. There is a good chance that such depression can be treated successfully, although some people may be liable to a recurrence.

Most people whom you are likely to be called upon to help will be at the point of the continuum where it is relatively easy to link lowered mood to an event in the person's life. Whilst time itself helps to ameliorate such a condition, good counselling will assist the process.

Depression may be characterized by moroseness, lack of energy, feelings of self-reproach, and a tendency to dwell on unpleasant aspects of life. Some people may become very unhappy indeed and show signs of morbid thinking and despair. Some may become so desperate that they attempt suicide. Suicide attempts are sufficiently important to have warranted a separate section of this book (pp. 35–6). Occasionally young people hide their deeper and softer feelings of dejection and hopelessness by behaving in ways which appear to indicate that their mood is anything but one of depression. In this way drug-taking, heavy drinking, reckless risk-taking, and promiscuity may all conceal depression.

Depression can adversely affect intellectual and physical performance. Often the first signs you will notice will be a lack of concentration and underachieving. Complaints about aches and pains and insomnia are possible signs but they might equally relate to anxiety.

SUNDAYS CAME AROUND WITH DEPRESSING REGULARITY

How can you help?

You are aiming to help a dejected person recover confidence in being able to cope with difficulties. This may involve helping the person to face up to an unpleasant situation, or go through a period of mourning over some loss which was not properly dealt with when it occurred. It may also involve getting the person to focus on his or her achievements or assets rather than losses, regrets, and inadequacies. But your starting point is acceptance. It will help if the person has confidence that you are genuinely trying to appreciate what the situation feels like to them. For this reason it is unwise to come straight in with examples of the good things in the person's life or an assurance that everything is going to be fine. That is not the way it feels to the other person and you will lose many of your clients if you don't acknowledge the reality of their feelings at the beginning.

Once the person you are trying to help is confident that you are hearing what he or she is telling you about how he or she feels, you can begin to direct attention towards positive things. You will be working with him or her to concentrate less on morose ruminations and more on things that are going on in the environment and the needs of other people. To do this you will need to show the following attitudes:

Sensitivity to the real difficulties of the dejected person combined with gentle but firm rejection of inaccurate or exaggerated statements about people or events.

Confidence in the person's strengths—but only based on real knowledge of the person.

Support for attempts to face up to problems or emotions.

Encouragement for attempts to overcome the self-neglect which sometimes characterizes depression and to establish a healthy personal routine.

Optimism that the period of depression will end and that the person will soon be feeling positive and full of vigour.

If you begin by listening carefully and acknowledging the reality of a depressed person's feelings and then move on to a counselling role based on the positive approaches listed above, you should be able to move on to helping the person to plan ahead, tackle problems, and set goals. Your long-term aim is to restore confidence and energy. To do this you may rehearse difficult situations with the person and help him or her to practise a confident successful approach to them. Challenges which are not too unrealistic or threatening may help at this point. In general, the emphasis should be on strategies for future action, the success of which you might offer to help review. Throughout the whole time you are helping a person emerge from a lowered mood you will be doing anything you can to improve his or her self-respect. Moving gradually from positive reinforcement to practical goal-setting you have a good chance of helping a dejected person.

Anorexia nervosa

What is it?

Anorexia nervosa is a serious disorder which afflicts a small number of adolescent girls and young women. It is rare in boys. The sufferer refuses to eat sufficient food and frequently this results in severe emaciation. Anorectics are usually obsessed with their appearance and may insist that they are overweight, despite evidence to the contrary. Occasionally anorectics indulge in binge-eating as a way of inducing vomiting and thus *reducing* food intake.

It would appear that there is no single cause of anorexia nervosa, but it is noticeable that the condition is often associated with difficulty in coming to terms with adolescent maturation. Anxiety about separation from parental protection has often been noted. Anxiety about sexual development has been a feature of many cases and it is thought to be significant that among the consequences of extreme weight-loss are a cessation of menstruation and a body shape which looks more like that of a child than a young woman. The social preoccupation with slimness in females is an obvious contributing factor and many anorectics start out following a slimming diet and end up having to be hospitalized because of extreme weight-loss.

Most anorectics are of average or above-average intelligence and come from materially comfortable homes. The parents of many anorectics are well-qualified professional people. Academic pressures from parents who over-emphasize educational attainment may be an important component in a significant number of cases, as are conflicts within the family in other cases.

By the time that substantial weight-loss has occurred, anorectics are likely to look frail and ill and to feel the cold more than most people. On the other hand, they can often maintain an alertness which is surprising in the light of their emaciated state. There is a mortality rate of about 5%–10% of anorectics each year, and serious cases will almost certainly involve hospitalization. Bed-rest, a carefully regulated and supervised weight restoration programme, coupled with individual and family treatment, have a good chance of success.

How can you help?

Whatever the causes, anorexia nervosa is made worse by circumstances which cause anxiety about appearance, diet, and independence. Educators have a responsibility to ensure that young girls are not subjected to stress in these areas.

Before treatment and during rehabilitation, the best help you can give is straightforward sympathy. If you can achieve some kind of rapport with the person, that will obviously be beneficial, but it is unwise to make references to appearance even if you intend them positively. Direct answers to questions about health, diet, and physical development are helpful. If you think someone is under undue academic pressure, you would in any case seek to reduce the pressure. A practical approach to helping girls take on responsibility and accept growing up is of the utmost importance.

If you observe a girl with marked weight-loss and obvious disturbance of her normal eating pattern, you should use the referral system which operates in your establishment to ensure that her condition is not overlooked.

Suicide and self-harm

What lies behind attempted suicide?

The peak age for attempted suicide is between 20 and 30 but the age-range between 14 and 18 shows a high incidence in this country. The actual intentions of a person who attempts suicide are not easy to gauge. It is probable that among young people, relatively few will have made a determined decision to end their lives. They may have wanted an end to their problems rather than an end to their lives. They frequently leave open the possibility that someone will intervene in time to save them. They may want to cause regret in other people. In some young people suicide attempts are modelled on the way in which other members of the family have responded to difficulties, and thoughts about outcome are very vague. There is often ambivalence about dying. The reasons why someone attempts suicide are also very various. In some cases life is simply unbearable. In others a sudden extreme of mood is so strong that suicide is attempted on impulse. All self-harming episodes should be taken seriously. Neither the degree of skill shown by the person attempting suicide nor the severity of the harm are an indication of the seriousness of the person's emotional problems. If someone tries to harm him or herself this represents a powerful communication.

Action on discovering a suicide attempt

Apply first aid (see pp. 73–7) to stop haemorrhage and clear airways. If the person is unconscious, lie him or her in the recovery position. If the person is conscious, check what he or she has done. Very occasionally people use more than one method of suicide. Remove the possibility of further self-harm but do not interfere with any substances associated with suicidal action. Make it clear to the person that you are going to keep him or her safe and prevent any further self-harm. Make the person comfortable. Get medical and whatever other help you feel is appropriate.

What can you do to help a person who has recently attempted suicide?

You are not going to be the only person trying to help a person who has recently attempted suicide. Find out, discreetly, what other help is being offered and make sure you don't undermine it.

By and large your efforts will be confined to making life as secure and bearable for the person as you can. Do not allow yourself to be blackmailed by threats of further suicide attempts but *do* pay attention to what the person is saying about his or her circumstances. If you are asked for help check out how this is to be handled with any therapist who is also involved. Suicide is the manifestation of a number of emotional conditions and not a condition in itself. There are, therefore, no specific approaches for counselling people who have attempted suicide. On the other hand there are one or two considerations which you may find it helpful to keep in mind.

Although self-harming is to be taken seriously this does not mean that you should look for some major disaster or set of extreme circumstances in the person's life. People do sometimes over-react and act impulsively even to the point of endangering their lives.

Avoid complicated arguments about the right to live or die. You may have feelings or strong beliefs about this issue but they are unlikely to be helpful to someone who is distressed.

Be prepared for expressions of anger as well as despair. Not infrequently suicide is an attempt to hurt other people.

In general the guidelines for counselling and the notes on depression and anxiety in this book are an appropriate background for offering help to someone who has been involved in a suicide attempt or self-harming episode.

Disruptive behaviour—the persistent disrupter

Identifying disruptive behaviour

People from all social groupings, races, ability ranges, and age groups can be disruptive. There is no 'disruptive type' of person in the strict sense. It is easy to see how certain social conditions increase the likelihood of people behaving in unhelpful ways, but there is no set of social conditions which guarantees bad behaviour. You will have noted that adult groups (such as committees, boards of governors, staff groups) have their disruptive members. There may well be some contexts in which you are, or could become, the disruptive member.

There is an infinite variety of behaviours which can disrupt a group. Some are passive (e.g. non-cooperation, extreme inattention); some are aggressive (e.g. threatening, violence, mockery). Given this variety and the variety of factors in the life of the disrupter which have contributed to his or her attitude, there will never be a cure-all for disruption.

Interesting, and occasionally useful, though speculation about the cause of disruptive behaviour may be, your first task is to clarify 'what' not 'why'. You have to clarify:

—what actual behaviour is at issue;
—what exact effect the behaviour is having;
—who is being adversely affected by it;
—what or who can be changed to alleviate the situation.

You are weighing up these factors against a background of conflicting loyalty. You have regard for the disrupter as an individual who is in your

'Arson in the chemmy lab, drugs in the loo, CSE results down the drain – and you are the man to sort it all out – now go out there and knock 'em dead.'

care. You have regard also for a whole group for whom you have responsibility. How you deal with this conflict is going to decide your general approach to the situation.

Analysing disruptive behaviour

You have to decide what is actually going on. Don't just let a heading go up in your mind. There are some questions to be asked before you take action.

1. *What* is it that is being said, done, or left undone that you are labelling as disruptive?
2. *Where* is it happening? Does this person always behave like this in this environment? Is this the only environment where the person behaves like this?
3. *When* does the behaviour which is causing you concern occur? What time of day, stage of term or course? How long does the behaviour last?
4. *Who* needs to be around when this person behaves this way? Are you concerned with a dramatization (that is, a behaviour pattern which needs an audience)? Does the audience participate? Do they make matters worse? Does this person behave badly with other groups? Is there a difference between the way this person behaves with adults and peers?

Evaluating the disruptive behaviour

Having pinned down *what* the behaviour is which is causing you concern you need to establish *why* this behaviour is worrying you. What effect is the behaviour having on other people and the environment? Who is being affected and what effect does the behaviour have on them? Don't forget to scrutinize your own reactions with the same vigour as those of colleagues and other students. You may find that the behaviour is reminding you of unpleasant experiences of your own. It would be very understandable if your own worries and irritations were re-kindled by disruptive behaviour, but in evaluating the seriousness of the behaviour you have somehow to disentangle your own personal history from the situation.

Examine the norms against which you are assessing the behaviour. It is possible that these norms are outmoded or reflect unnecessary inhibitions. You will, in any case, have to identify the environment in which these norms apply. Is it the school as a whole, parts of the school, society, a particular environment?

The key question which remains is: what is going to happen if you do not intervene? By assessing the seriousness of the consequences of non-intervention in the light of the previous areas of enquiry, you will be able to decide how urgent intervention is. What you then have to decide is the likely effect of different kinds of intervention and to do this you must review what else you know about the disrupter.

Assessing the personality and capabilities of the disrupter

You need to establish what you know about this person so that you can gauge the effectiveness of possible strategies for intervening.

For a start why does this person turn up at school or club or college? There must be some kind of loyalty or dependence operating and this is important.

Does the disrupter realize what effect his or her behaviour is having? Do you think he or she realizes what it is you disapprove of?

How much control does this person have over his or her behaviour? Do you think he or she can change, and if so for how long?

What is the disrupter communicating about him or herself (or other people or the environment) by the disruptive behaviour? Is the message 'I'm bored', 'this place frustrates me', 'these people bother me', 'I'm lost', etc.?

Have you noticed the good behaviour in the disrupter? What clues does the good behaviour give you about the situation? What motivates the disrupter? What brings out his or her best behaviour?

Intervening

Having weighed up the behaviour, its effect, and the personality of the disrupter you decide to intervene. You will have decided who and what needs to change. In most situations some change will be needed from several people, and possibly the system, if disruptive behaviour is to be successfully interrupted, modified, or accommodated.

Has the environment got to change?
The environment means the physical environment and the institutional rules and regulations. You will want to look at the routine that is expected of this person, and the groups he or she is in. You will have examined whether there are environments which are conducive to good behaviour in this person and considered whether he or she can spend more time in them or whether other environments can be made more like them.

Have other people got to change?
Are there individuals or groups who are making things difficult for this person? Are there people aiding and abetting the bad behaviour? Don't leave yourself out. You may be making matters worse. You may even be the cause of the problem. It is very likely that whatever changes are needed from the disrupter you too will have to change. It is very difficult to achieve change in someone if you are not prepared to reciprocate that change.

Effecting change
Work out whether you are planning for a complete end to the disruptive behaviour, some modification, or ways of accommodating it. Work out also what time scale you are working to and who your allies are in effecting change.

Changing the environment
Temporary changes of environment to interrupt disruptive behaviour are a well-tried method. A time-out room away from normal groups is a good idea. It should be supervised by a member of staff who has no disciplinary problems. It is unlikely to help if the atmosphere is punitive; a silent purposeful environment allows cooling-off time. Disrupters can be removed to such an environment to stabilize sessions and long-term tactics worked out later.

In the long term it may well help if the disrupter is given some power to change his or her own environment in negotiation with you. Try reviewing the places where this person has to work and play. In the same spirit a review of what is compulsory and what is voluntary in the personal programme of the disrupter is likely to be useful. Perhaps the balance needs shifting one way or the other.

Changing groups
You may have to help groups to look at behaviour in relation to disrupters. If they are aiding and abetting out of fear you will need to make them take a more courageous stand. If they sympathize with the negative feelings of the disrupter, involve them in the programme for tackling the things which upset the disrupter. You don't want a lynch-mob but you do want groups which accept responsibility for the behaviour of their members and this is a difficult lesson for many groups to learn. You may, of course, have to change the membership of some groups before improvements are possible.

Negotiating change
In effect you are negotiating a contract for change. This contract will have no weight if it is not clear. To begin with you have to communicate exactly what improvements in behaviour you regard as necessary. Check that you have been understood. Make it quite clear by all your dealings with the disrupter that what you are rejecting is a set of behaviours and not the person him or herself. If you cannot do this you will not be able to make a meaningful contract with this person. Make visible to the person what effects the behaviour is having and why it matters.

Agree targets for change and include change in your own behaviour. Make sure these targets are realistic. Agree a timescale and ensure that it is fully understood how progress is to be monitored. Outline the support that will be given. Make clear what will happen next if the improvements do not happen (but not as a threat). Make full use of incentives and stress the reciprocity of the contract. Negotiate the whole thing in a spirit of trust and optimism.

What if your strategies fail?
Schools normally have a standard referral system whereby Educational Psychologists become involved with students. They will help you with strategies which keep the student in school. If these strategies fail they will have a range of options to recommend which may include home tuition, transfer to another school, complete or part withdrawal to a special unit, or withdrawal to a psychiatric unit. In some areas there are family and adolescent units for short-stay or day attendance. Your opinion should be asked about the most appropriate way of helping the disrupter. It may be useful if you maintain contact and provide continuity in the person's educational life.

Your institution should have a well worked-out progression of strategies for dealing with difficult young people. This progression should be understood by all the staff. This will help to ensure that arbitrary, haphazard, over-reactive, and generally inappropriate responses to disruptive behaviour are minimized. It will also help to ensure that conflicting strategies are not in operation. To deal effectively with disruptive behaviour you and your colleages need to know what is expected of you and what resources you have at your disposal. From the point of view of the young people it is helpful for them to know that there are no 'sudden death' aspects of the way they will be treated so that they feel that change is possible and worthwhile.

Final caution
Avoid any strategy which makes it impossible for all concerned to emerge with dignity. Humiliation is a defensive weapon frequently used by harassed teachers. In the long term it is counter-productive. The vast majority of disruptive behaviour comes from people with an impaired sense of their own worth. Don't make matters worse by further undermining their self-image.

Persistent non-attendance at school

Types of non-attendance

Persistent absence from school is likely to be for one or more of the following reasons:

1 The student is ill.
2 The parents of the student are keeping the student away from school.
3 The student is absent without the permission of parents (truancy).
4 The student refuses to go to school despite the encouragement of parents (school-refusing).

There are standard procedures for dealing with absenteeism through illness and there is no point in elaborating them here. The section in this book on dealing with parents (pp. 48–54) is probably the best guide for tackling cases where parents are withholding or frequently withdrawing students. It is worth mentioning here however that reasons for parents behaving in this way may be very complex and include such situations as:

a deeply felt religious, political, or cultural beliefs;
b the use of a young person as a surrogate parent in deprived or bereaved families;
c illegal under-age employment or enforced labour; this may be linked to cases of family hardship or to a traditional alternative view of the duties of children in society.

Truancy

The extent to which a young person has made a pre-meditated decision to be absent will vary enormously. In some cases elaborate steps will be taken to cover the fact of truancy. In others young people act on a whim after setting off with the full intention of reaching school. It is therefore essential for those who have responsibility for following up truancy to avoid generalizations and try to assess each individual case with the help of educational social workers.

Most truancy is sporadic even if it is persistent. Because it is disruptive and because it is seen as a rejection, schools tend to react summarily. Individual teachers may feel threatened by truants and become over-involved personally. This is despite the fact that feelings about teachers and school as such are only a part of the reason why most truants absent themselves. The majority of persistent truants are people who are not performing well at school, lack parental encouragement to improve, and have a variety of material or social problems unrelated to school. It is not uncommon for truants to be involved in petty crime but it by no means follows that they will be.

Some people do find school oppressive, boring, or irrelevant and make a conscious decision to give it a miss. Some people will be in the throes of a disagreement with those in authority. Not everyone who feels bored or fed up with school plays truant and it is relevant to examine the development of a sense of loyalty and responsibility in truants. Without commenting on the quality of our schools it is worth noting that research into the backgrounds of truants shows a high incidence of irresponsible parental attitudes to employment and authority. Equally if parents have had a boring or generally unsuccessful schooling their attitude to compulsory education is likely to be ambivalent if not openly hostile. They will have considerable influence over their children. It is likely that there are many thousands of young people in this country who feel only loosely committed to full-time education and who can easily be deterred or distracted from it.

What can you do?

Every school should have a non-punitive but efficient system for following up absenteeism. The main features of such a system should include:

1. Always following up absenteeism as fast as possible.
2. Using an inter-professional network to investigate the circumstances of each individual truant.
3. Attempting to distinguish between those factors which initiate truancy and those which perpetuate it.
4. Avoiding measures which hinder or prevent communication (such as suspension).

5 Communicating clearly the reasons why it is important for a person to attend school apart from academic progress. In addition to the legal obligation, these centre around the social need for integration with peers, access to adult support and guidance, and learning how to face difficulties and fulfil obligations. All of these are important as preparation for a variety of adult roles.

6 Respecting the importance of the life young people live outside school, its pressures, obligations, and benefits.

In tackling truancy you will often be confronting difficult aspects of our society such as prejudice, material disadvantage, cultural alienation, criminal subcultures, cruelty, and exploitation. Often the best you can do is to help ensure that the school environment is as free of these difficulties as possible, that all students have your respect, that they know that truancy will be pursued vigorously according to a clear system which has been explained to all, and that the curriculum is as relevant to the needs of individuals as you can help to make it.

School-refusing

In this book the term 'school-refusing' is used to describe the situation where a person has developed such a fear of school that ordinary attempts to enforce attendance have been unsuccessful. The degree of irrationality of the fear will vary and at one extreme there may be people suffering from phobic anxiety states which include an irrational fear of school. Many school-refusers can be seen to be reacting, perhaps over-reacting, to problems which can be identified. Changing the situation to remedy these problems, however, may not have much impact on the school-refuser. Once a serious fear of school has developed it will take a careful programme of action to help a person readjust and attend regularly.

Some school-refusers become physically ill at the prospect of attending school. Headaches, vomiting, and various aches and pains are common. Many school-refusers show an intention to attend school but are then unable to fulfil it. Often they come from homes where parental encouragement to attend school and perform well are strong. School-refusers mostly have no previous record of non-conforming, are of average to above-average intelligence, and have been doing quite well at school prior to the episode of school-refusing. This contrasts them fairly sharply with the typical truant.

The factors associated with school-refusing go beyond the student's situation at school. Very often the reaction to school is nothing more than an indication that there are more general problems. Where there are actual school problems contributing to the person's condition they include such things as:

1 Fear of oppression by other school students. Here one has to be careful about which came first, the student's emotional disorder (identified by unsympathetic peers), or the oppressive treatment.

2 A feeling that the school has not recognized some learning difficulties with which the student is struggling.
3 Undue parental or other adult pressure to 'do well' at school.
4 Reaction to unfavourable comparisons made between the student's performance at school and that of siblings.
5 Fear of a relationship with a particular teacher. This may reflect genuine unfair treatment, or a long-standing misinterpretation of the way the teacher relates to the student.
6 Social embarrassment at having to perform certain tasks at school which might reveal aspects of physical development about which the student is uncertain or distressed. The typical example here would be communal showers around the time of early pubertal development or the onset of menstruation.

School-refusers are very often insecure about any kind of change in daily routine and have general problems about being separated from their families even for short periods of time. Sometimes the transition from primary to secondary education has been traumatic.

What can you do to help?

It is likely that a school-refuser will be receiving help from someone. There are many approaches to rehabilitation but they all involve a carefully planned strategy which exposes the young person to school in a progressive series of stages. Psychiatric teams will discuss with the appropriate teachers what the strategy is and the part they are to play.

Some school-refusing might be averted if the transitional stages of education were clearer and more sensitively handled. Excessive accentuation of academic performance coupled with failure to identify learning problems should be remedied. Continuity of teachers and a minimizing of changes of routine are helpful in averting anxieties about change. A recognition of the sensitivity of adolescents to their physical development would make life more bearable for a large number of young people and might avert a few instances of school-refusing.

It is important to note that helping a person to overcome a school-refusing episode has implications far beyond their success at school. The ability of the person to face up to new situations and act independently is at stake. School-refusing may become work-refusing or the refusal to face the responsibilities of parenthood and citizenship. In some cases a chronic condition might set in which permanently disables the person. It is for this reason that most psychiatrists make swift and determined efforts to re-integrate the student and deal with the fears which surrounded the refusal to attend.

4 The sexuality of young people

General difficulties

The majority of young people still learn most about sex from their peers and find this unsatisfactory. They want authoritative information from parents and those adults with responsibility for their welfare.

There are still too few localities where young people can guarantee to get good sex education. School and youth group provision varies from year to year as well as from group to group. Many boys' schools have no provision at all.

Even parents who regard it as their responsibility (rather than that of the school or youth group) often fail to carry out sex education. This may well be because both parents and their adolescent children require a degree of privacy from one another.

There is a destructive myth (reinforced by some educational spokesmen) that instruction about sex actually promotes early intercourse. The people who believe this have not worked in clinics or as psychosexual counsellors. There is ample evidence that the exact opposite is the case. On the whole young people who have been able to discuss sex and contraception with parents or other responsible adults start intercourse later and use contraception more effectively.

The effect of explicit sex scenes in films and on TV has been widely debated. Moralists often fail to grasp the fact that the advertisers with their direct targeting and stereotyping are giving far more confusing messages than most film dramas. Good teenage magazines are careful not to include advertising which is confusing or inflammatory but not all the magazines are good. On the other hand clear unbiased information about contraception is still forbidden on the radio and television.

What can you do to help?

Relieve the peer group of the task of giving accurate information about sex. If you do not feel able to supply the information yourself, make sure that the young people and their parents know where the information is to be obtained.

Avoid sly references to sex and confusing sexual jokes.

If someone comes to you with specific worries about contraception or pregnancy, do not hesitate to refer them to the family planning services. It is responsible to make such referrals and it does not subvert parental authority. Indeed, a clinic consultation frequently helps to open up and improve communication within a family. Most young people who attend clinics have been at risk of unwanted pregnancy for some time already. Some are already pregnant. By referring, you are doing the most effective thing you can to diminish the risk to the young person.

Young people who seek advice about contraception are sometimes seeking support to withstand unwelcome peer pressure towards sexual activity. This is an important possibility to bear in mind.

Remember that unwanted pregnancy is only one hazard of early sexual intercourse. Sexually transmitted diseases are on the increase and the risk of cancer of the cervix later in life is definitely raised. This is not mentioned so that you can wag the finger at young people but in order to indicate the urgency of good, informed sexual counselling and advice. Unless you have a qualification in gynaecology or training in psychosexual counselling, the chances are that there are people on hand in your area who are in a better position than you are to deal with the sexual queries and worries of young people. Please use them.

Teenage pregnancy

You may not like the word 'teenage' but the point is this: a girl under the age of 17 who becomes pregnant is putting her own and her baby's health at a higher risk than a girl over the age of 17. Unwanted pregnancies also have a higher health risk than planned ones.

Some points to bear in mind when dealing with a young pregnant girl:

1 Referral is not just advisable, it is *inevitable*. This person needs medical care straight away. Many girls conceal their condition until it is too late to terminate the pregnancy. Pregnancy tests are best done by a Family Planning Clinic (or Young People's Advisory Clinic), or through a GP. All such tests are confidential.

2 In addition to her medical care it is very important that the girl continues to have access to her chosen confidante throughout pregnancy and *most importantly after the birth*.

3 If the baby is kept, support should continue as long after the birth as possible. At first the small baby and the attention it attracts may obscure the extent of responsibility the mother has undertaken. When the baby starts making more demands it ceases to be merely an 'animated doll' and the pressures on the young mother may become unbearable, especially with her peers continuing to enjoy a normal unfettered social life.

3 If the pregnancy is lost, a period of mourning has to be gone through whether the loss was chosen or not. This applies also when a baby is given for adoption.

4 Family support is the best outcome. More often than you might imagine families come through their initial distress and anger over teenage pregnancy and rally round. Do not give up hope of this happening and do what you can to encourage it.

5 If the girl is at school, she should be welcomed back if she is prepared to return. If not she should be helped to continue her education elsewhere. The

disruption or loss of her education is the most severe and permanent penalty which can befall a school-aged mother.

6 Do not make any inferences about the character of a girl from the fact of an unwanted pregnancy. Well-intentioned but trusting and naive girls are as much at risk as precociously explorative or irresponsible girls. Pregnancy can result from a single act of indiscretion and anyone can be exploited. It is also worth mentioning that the number of promiscuous (a term we ought perhaps to scrap in any case) girls is considerably smaller than gutter journalism suggests. Where it occurs, promiscuity is a sign of serious anxiety deserving of compassion, not recrimination.

Don't forget the father. Too little constructive attention is paid to young putative fathers. They are either condemned or ignored altogether. This is despite the fact that they may be extremely frightened, confused, or full of remorse. If you are able to talk to the father it is important to check what support *he* needs.

Sexually transmitted diseases

The only thing these different diseases have in common is that they are transmitted almost exclusively by genital contact. Not all sexually transmitted diseases are very serious, but among them are diseases which will cause permanent and serious damage in their advanced stages. Some of the diseases can be transmitted genetically to children. The symptoms of the minor and serious diseases are often similar. In this field of medicine a little knowledge, leading to wrong advice, can have very serious consequences. For this reason no attempt is made here to distinguish the various diseases, but clinics will supply leaflets on request. If a young person comes to you asking advice about the symptoms listed below you should do your utmost to persuade him or her to go as soon as possible to a GP or a Special Clinic and cease sexual contact until the results of tests are known. The Special Clinics will observe strict confidentiality and will not even inform parents against the client's wishes.

The following symptoms do not necessarily indicate a sexually transmitted disease, but they do indicate the risk of one in a sexually active person. Treatment in the early stages is almost always successful, quick, and painless. The risk is not worth taking. A check-up is the common-sense responsible action to recommend.

Boys Pain in passing urine
Discharge from the penis
Sores on, or near, the genitals (which may or may not be painful)

Girls Pain in passing urine
Genital sores
Genital irritation

Vaginal discharge (in excess of normal discharge). With girls who have only recently reached puberty, this symptom is difficult to assess since they may not yet know what normal discharge is like.

Unfortunately girls can have quite advanced stages of some of these diseases before any symptoms appear. They are also most vulnerable to the severe effects of several of these diseases. For this reason, and because of the extreme contagiousness of some of the diseases, it is essential that people who have had sexually transmitted diseases confirmed by a doctor and clinic make sure that their partner(s) attend for a check-up as soon as possible. This is a delicate matter and considerable counselling skill may be required to enable a young person to act responsibly and confront or name sexual partners. Special Clinics employ trained social workers to counsel clients attending. Clinics would rather see large numbers of people who turn out not to have a sexually transmitted disease than miss even small numbers of people who have. The treatment is usually a course of antibiotics and will not normally prevent the young person from attending school, college, or youth group.

5 Home problems

Difficulties with parents

General relationship between educators and parents

If you only get to know parents when their children are in difficulties you are going to be at a disadvantage. Whatever the organization you work for, there ought to be some way in which parents and staff can meet on equal terms. Many schools and youth organizations encourage parents to take an interest in their affairs. Knowing the parents can help you to help the children.

Your dealings with parents are fraught with difficulty. You cannot hide behind the normal barriers which protect professionals. Parents have been through many years of schooling and may also have been to college or belonged to youth organizations. They claim inside knowledge of your profession. You may be *in loco parentis* during certain hours of certain days but the European Court recently ruled that you have to discharge that responsibility in keeping with the kind of parenting the children are receiving at home. But how can you hope to know what kind of parenting that is—until it is too late?

Parents know more about their children than you do but you know things which they don't. Some of the things known uniquely are likely to surprise the other party. Parenting is a basic widespread area of human responsibility in which you, as a private individual, have your own expertise and inadequacy. When you meet a parent you may be meeting on several levels at once. Your relationship with a parent may be:

one caring adult to another
parent to parent
professional to parent
professional to professional.

Extra clarity and intelligence are going to be needed if you are to communicate usefully. It is going to help tremendously if you have a varied and ongoing relationship with parents.

There are two basic ways in which you may become involved with the difficulties people are having with their parents. The first is where young people come to you and report difficulties they are having at home. The second is where a distressed parent comes to see you.

Responding to young people who may be having difficulties with their parents

Most young people will eventually leave home. In that sense difficulties with parents are nearly always going to be temporary. On the other hand the way families behave has a lasting effect on the kind of independent life people are able to establish. Your role is to enable young people to understand and cope with their own family situations.

1 Try to remain impartial. Remember that you only have part of the picture. Don't instantly set up battle stations against the parents. Remember also that parents of teenagers are going to be aged (on average) between 35 and 50 and may be in the throes of a mid-life crisis themselves. Their assumptions about their marriage, career, health, and capabilities may well be being tested, as the parameters of their lives become clearer. Their young adult children will be contributing to this testing but may not be thanked for it.

   Your own experiences as a child, and possibly as a parent, will tend to distort your judgement of what you are being told. Each family is unique. It has its own rules, power structure, emergency routines, sense of drama, alliances, hopes, and expectations. Just because the way a family is said to carry on appears weird to you does not mean to say that the family is inadequate or unviable as a unit. Somehow you have got to extend your frame of reference and imagine the viability of some family structures and beliefs which upset you. There is no such thing as a typical family. There is no single model of the coping or caring family.

2 Distinguish facts from feelings. Don't get carried away by drama or invective. You should be able to picture for yourself how the intensity of family life distorts issues and even memories of what has been said or done. Like the rest of us, young people will tend to exaggerate and over-generalize what is happening to them at home. They may lead you to believe that the whole family is against them, for instance, whereas there may actually be no concensus in the family at all. Try to break down the situation into facts and feelings and give each the appropriate attention.

3 Don't underestimate family loyalty. Some young people are verbally completely dismissive of their parents. There is much evidence to show that even the most apparently hardened people go on being influenced by their parents well past the age of maturity. Despite rhetoric, family loyalty is strong, however oppressive parents may be. Even if a person does have to separate from parents who have been extreme in their thoughtlessness or cruelty, that person will nearly always suffer a crisis of conscience about leaving.

4 Never recommend splitting a family without referring to people with specialist knowledge of families. It takes deep inside knowledge coupled with specialist training to identify a family which should be split because it can't cope with all its members. There is general agreement among specialists with responsibility for making such judgements that splitting a family, even temporarily, is absolutely the last resort after other strategies have failed. It is, of course, true that young people deserve protection from oppressive and grossly inconsistent parents, but never act unilaterally on this issue. Consult and refer. Check your spoken and written judgements very carefully.

5 Keep in mind long-term aims. You have been approached by a particular person who is experiencing difficulties. You have to decide whether the

difficulties can actually be removed, and if so, what needs to be done. In most cases they cannot be removed. They may be ameliorated or they may have to be coped with as they are. Either way your aim is to enable the young person to cope. If it is a question of communicating to parents the effect their behaviour is having, you might think you can put this to them better than a less articulate or anxious child. You may want to take on the role of interpreter: but bear in mind that you will have helped with only one set of circumstances. You may not be there to interpret the next time. It may be far more helpful in the long run if you can enable the young person to communicate directly.

Responding to the distressed parent

The professional educator is seen as being in a special position with special powers. In the course of your career you can expect to be confronted by adults who are distressed for reasons which have nothing to do with you or your dealings with their children. Yet the way they confront you may be very personal. You are going to have to be honest with yourself and the parent. Can you really offer anything more than normal social sympathy? Your loyalty, through your professional commitment, is to the child. That is where your focus should be in the first instance. You may have to refer the parent to someone who has the time and the expertise to respond in depth.

Dealing with an angry parent

Dealing with anger is one of the hardest tasks. If a parent shouts at you or shows other kinds of aggression the chances are that you will find it hard really to take in what is being said. You may even go quite numb and feel unable to proceed. (This may be how young people feel when you shout at or threaten them!) Here are some suggestions which may help you to deal with an angry parent:

1. Don't take it personally. You may have done something which was wrong or needs changing; but it may not really be you that is being shouted at. You represent authority. You may link parents with unpleasant memories of oppressive school days. You may be the one accessible part of a system which makes the parent feel powerless. Policemen, traffic wardens, health visitors, receptionists, and local government officers get the same treatment frequently. So don't go straight into a personal defence.
2. Aim to defuse the attack—not to deflect it. People who let their emotions lead their actions make sudden shifts of position which can be just as alarming as the situation they first present to you. For instance, it is quite common for the enraged parent, who came to 'sort you out' because of the way you are said to have treated a child, suddenly to switch the anger in the direction of the child on hearing your side of things. If the child gets beaten up because you made a good defence of your actions, you are partly responsible.

3 Anger may be the most obvious sign of distress but behind it may lie great areas of fear and misery. By using some of the approaches suggested in the section in this book on counselling you may be able to encourage the person to express some of these feelings.
4 Work out whether you are going to tackle *issues* or *feelings*. You can only tackle issues if some kind of sensible communication is possible. If this is so, try to establish what concrete issues can be discussed. If it is a dispute over something you have done, find out what the parent would have expected you to do. Explore alternatives—admit that they exist unless you are 100% sure that they do not.
5 Try to move to an unthreatening environment. If sensible communication is impossible it may be partly because of the environment in which you are meeting. Not only are you on home ground, but it is ground which has strong associations for parents. You have two main choices: either you try to move the meeting to a less formal environment which may be neutral or home ground for the parent; or you may decide that the nature of the situation is such that a more formal meeting is called for and arrange to involve colleagues or refer the case to independent persons.

Visiting families

You should not automatically assume that you are called upon to intervene personally in family crises or difficulties, however much you may want to sort things out. Sometimes, however, you may decide that a visit to the family is appropriate and you will want to plan such a visit very carefully.

To begin with you need to consider your assumptions about the family. Your aim is to help people to communicate and co-operate—in other words, to open up possibilities. You cannot do this if you are carrying with you negative assumptions. Proceed on the assumption that the parents are doing the best they can at this point in time, however awful things seem to be. Don't go in assuming that you can identify guilt, inadequacy, or deliberate malevolence. We all do the best we can as parents, but we are hampered by the lasting effect of unhelpful things that were done to us. This doesn't mean parents can't or shouldn't change their ways. It just means that blaming and reproach are pointless. The parents may have been excellent with the children when small and only really hit difficulties with them as adolescents. There may be pressures on the family you do not know about. You need to check out your prejudices and open your mind before the visit.

You also need to be clear about the role you are going to adopt. Are you going as an arbitrator, an observer, a messenger, or a representative? This is not an exhaustive list, of course. In most cases your best stance is probably as one who seeks to find out rather than one who intends to change everything. You can be quite determined in an investigative role and you may see an opening for direct influence at a later stage.

Encouraging negotiation
If there is a family difficulty, communication is not enough. What is required is agreement for change, however slight. Remember that negotiation may be new to some families. You have a very short time to try and teach some basic negotiating skills.

Try to have all parties present in a negotiation. Children and parents may be embarrassed by this idea, but press for it. It is better, for instance, to be alongside a youngster who has to confront parents than acting as a stand-in. Check that everybody is getting a chance to be heard and go back over ground yourself if you think someone was ignored. Act as a referee if necessary. Defer head-on conflict and don't allow brow-beating. If people keep hammering home the same opinion, point this out and encourage them to move on to another issue or a new way of looking at the original one. Go for workable compromises, not conversions.

Acting as a go-between
Sometimes teachers and youthworkers find themselves in a situation where direct communication has broken down between a young person and his or her parents. You may find yourself the only channel through which a family can reach one of its members. This is a very difficult role and you need to make clear how long and under what terms you will fulfil it. If it is a situation where you know the whereabouts of a child and the parents do not, you are likely to be regarded as both a threat and a source of hope. Great tact, reassurance, and clarity are required of you. Here is a short list of suggestions which have proved helpful to others in this situation:

1 Do not take sides or enter disputes.
2 Carry clear messages only. Work with each side until messages are clear.
3 Take messages in person whenever possible. Telephone intermediaries have sinister associations. In any case you should be working towards a situation where people confront each other personally and you will find it extremely difficult to promote this if you do not model what is required.
4 Do not react to threats at all, whether they are directed at you, the other party, or are self-destructive.
5 Be reliable. Don't add to the fear and suspicion.
6 Continually check the legal implications of what you are doing.
7 Keep a colleague informed. This should be a condition of accepting the role. You need support and you need to cover yourself against possible misinterpretation.

General considerations
Be realistic about what you can achieve. Family conflicts can be resolved, but the underlying reasons for them are more difficult to tackle. Remember you are coming into a unit which has a long history and a very complex structure.

Family therapists point out that families work in concert to maintain certain difficulties. If for instance there is a member of the family who is getting the thin end of the wedge and someone succeeds in making life more bearable for him or her, the power structure of the family has been shifted. But very frequently all that happens is that the oppression is focused on another member of the family. It has even been shown that predisposition to illness can shift around a family if the root cause of the family distress is not tackled successfully. The best you can do may be to improve coping skills and acceptance of difficulties. Even progress on that level is worth the effort you are putting in.

In all dealings with parents, remember that no one *owns* a child—not parents, not teachers, not youthworkers, no one. Children are their own people and this fact is not altered by the legal and moral obligations which others may have for protecting and nurturing them.

Accommodation

Despite a few isolated imaginative schemes, most areas are experiencing an ever-worsening problem with homelessness and accommodation stresses among young people. Recent legislation has tightened up on the rights and responsibilities of landlords and tenants alike, but unfortunately the average accommodation problem is not a legal but a logistic matter. This book cannot guide your dealings with logistical problems very closely but here is a checklist to help you to assess the situation and avoid embarrassing action. An outline of the main legal situations is given on pp. 103–6.

Some general points to note when dealing with someone who expresses an accommodation problem

1. Keep things in perspective. Accommodation crises frequently appear hopeless or desperate. Break the problem down into its component parts. Work on the practical issues as far as possible.
2. Don't jump to conclusions. Check the facts carefully. Shelter is a basic human need and as such an emotive issue. You may not be in receipt of the full story.
3. Don't look for villains. The Bad Landlord is a stock drama character. Sometimes the landlord's version of the story is rather different. There is no shortage of genuinely bad or unhelpful landlords but don't let that cloud the issue.
4. Get your priorities right. For example: there may be a legal point to pursue in the long run, but meanwhile where is your client going to sleep?
5. Check local variations. There are certain basic inalienable laws regarding tenancy but there are also a great many local rules, regulations, and resources. Try to check them out.

6 Don't accept responsibility for re-housing someone without careful thought. You will wish to help but you should be careful about giving the impression that you are taking over responsibility for the situation. There are many distressing cases of homelessness or oppressive tenancy but they are not helped by adults who shield young people from their responsibilities as tenants or accommodation seekers. Give support, but leave the responsibility where it belongs. For people under 16 the main responsibility lies with their parents unless a court has taken over that responsibility.

7 Get help for cases of homelessness. Unless you happen to own a small palace you are going to need to involve other people in cases of genuine homelessness. Most areas have emergency facilities for the homeless and all areas have information services.

8 Continue contact. Temporary or emergency accommodation can be depressing and isolating. It can be very useful for people in such situations to have regular informal contact with a responsible and caring adult.

Sometimes people are so relieved to have found accommodation for someone that they don't really investigate what sort of environment the person is now in. There are also, unfortunately, too many people who are happy to exploit those who are desperate for accommodation, especially if they are young and/or hard up. Your intervention could prevent exploitation. Your visits could put an end to it if it has begun. But again, get help if you can.

9 Remember what the long-term aim is. The person you are helping needs to find a safe, healthy, and secure place to live. Equally, he or she needs to develop the skills, responsibilities, and resources which will ensure that he or she can arrange such accommodation without help. Some people need considerable support while acquiring such assets.

6 Drugs

General background information

What are drugs?

Any substance which (by its chemical action) alters the way a person's body works is a potential drug. Another way of looking at it is that drugs are poisons for which a medicinal or social use has been found.

This is a drug culture: we are all part of it. Some drugs are so habitual to our culture that we tend to forget that they are drugs. Nicotine (from cigarettes), tannin and caffeine (from beverages such as tea and coffee), and alcohol are very commonly used drugs. Their use is recreational and social rather than medicinal. Aspirin and paracetamol are quite powerful drugs for which no prescription is required. Valium is one of the most commonly prescribed drugs throughout the western world. A vast promotional machine ensures that we are constantly self-prescribing various drugs either for pleasure or for the alleviation of minor ailments.

All drugs have their dangers and to some extent it is arbitrary which ones are legal and which not. If medical experts were asked to shortlist destructive drugs with a view to legislation against their uncontrolled use, they might well put alcohol on their list and omit one or two drugs which are currently illegal. Historically we have been extremely inconsistent about the legality of drugs.

Why are drugs taken?

Drugs may be used to:

help the body fight infection
relieve pain
change moods
remedy an impairment

How do drugs work?

The body's different systems can be compartmentalized crudely as follows:

respiratory	(breathing)
circulatory	(blood)
nervous	(messages)
digestive	(processing food)
muscular	(movement)
skeletal	(form structure and movement)
reproductive	

These systems are linked. All drugs will inevitably have side-effects because they always go through more than one of the body's systems. For example:

We take an aspirin to dull pain in the muscular system.

The drug goes first into the **digestive system** where it irritates the stomach lining.
It goes next through the **circulatory system** where it thins the blood.
Finally it reaches the **nervous system** where it turns off messages to the **muscular system** and alleviates the pain to which it was directed.
Unfortunately it also turns off other messages, some of which might be rather urgent.

You can see that our reason for taking a drug does not limit its effect. This is where the risk element comes in. The so-called abuse of drugs arises out of people being more interested in the side-effects than the main effect for which the drug was developed. For recreational purposes it is the effect of drugs on the nervous system which is paramount.

Grouping types of drugs

We can categorize drugs conveniently by the nature of their effect. This gives us three broad categories:

stimulants
depressants
hallucinogens

The Misuse of Drugs Act 1971 lists all the illegal drugs and divides them into three classes, in order of what it regards as their harmfulness.

Class A (carrying the highest penalties) includes drugs which used to be referred to as narcotics—opium, morphine, heroin, and cocaine. It includes preparations of any drugs intended for injections. It also includes LSD.

Class B includes cannabis and cannabis derivatives. It also includes oral amphetamines.

Class C includes Mandrax and certain stimulants not covered in class B.

The idea of classifying drugs in terms of harmfulness is fraught with difficulties but because you will still hear people referring to 'hard drugs' and 'narcotics' this section deals with them as a group, despite the fact that they can be divided among the three main categories already listed. Solvents and alcohol are depressants but their social implications demand that they be considered separately. Thus this section, as a whole, is divided into:

hard drugs or narcotics
stimulants
depressants
hallucinogens
solvents
alcohol.

Some practical suggestions for dealing with all kinds of drug abuse

Don't over-react.	Don't assume that anything drastic has to be done.
Safety first.	Remove the person from obvious danger before you do anything else. Remove the source of intoxication.
Assess the scene.	What drug has been taken—how much—how recently—by what method—for what reason?
Let people cry or shake.	Don't be afraid of the natural way in which human beings deal with distress.
Keep calm.	Don't get drawn into drama. Parents and other authority figures may over-react.
Stay humble but positive.	You want to help. You may need to assert discipline, but remember that the user may know more about the drug than you do.
First aid	The rules of first aid apply, especially those concerning unconsciousness. Lie an unconscious person in the recovery position to prevent choking. See section on First Aid (pp. 73–5).

Some suggestions for counselling and advice which apply to all drug abuse

Beware of moralization.	Drugs go in and out of fashion, and so do the reasons why people take them. It is not wicked to overdose or take drugs for kicks. It is not necessarily stupid either.
Keep your faith in the individual.	There is no inevitable or logical drug progression. People can and do dabble and come through. People can and do get deeply into drugs and come through.

Avoid generalizations.	Generalizations such as 'Drinking is bad for you' beg questions such as: how much? which drinks? when? where?
Check your facts.	Where are you getting your information? There are self-styled experts with axes to grind. The media feed on exaggeration.
Set a good example.	Don't preach abstinence from one drug if you are hooked on another. Do you slope off to the pub and get drunk after reading the riot act about sniffing glue? Is the staff room full of smoke at break time when the duty teacher is punishing the toilet fag club?
Avoid sensationalism.	Quite a lot of irresponsible drug use arises out of anxiety. Don't add to the anxiety. You may persuade someone to give up a relatively harmless habit only to drive them into a really self-destructive one.
Keep things in perspective.	Assess the scale of risk in a person's life-style. If a smoker is also a regular drunken driver you are wasting your time bothering him or her about the long-term effects of cigarettes.
Watch your language.	You say '____ing will make you ill'. The young people think of days off school, extra attention, no responsibilities. You say '____ing shortens your life'; they say 'Who wants to be old anyway?' You say '____ing is dangerous'; they associate danger with challenge, excitement, heroism. See section on dealing with risk (pp. 15–17).
Try a positive approach.	Warnings are notoriously hopeless, especially with young people. Your time may be better spent highlighting positive images of health; promoting self-esteem among your students; alleviating anxiety and boredom; and helping people to practise staying responsible while pursuing excitement and new experiences.

Keep your focus on the person.	People are more important than drugs. Don't get more interested in the substances than the people who are using them.
Protocol	Each institution will have its own rules and regulations for dealing with deviant behaviour. Whatever drug you are dealing with, you need to be aware of the institutional procedures required of you *before* you act. Don't wait for a crisis.

'Hard drugs' or narcotics

The law separates drugs into three main categories and this is the one that carries the heaviest penalties. All 'hard' drugs are widely used in medicine, usually as painkillers. All 'hard' drugs are expensive and you won't come across many users of the following unless something changes radically in the drug economy.

Cocaine—coke

What is it?	It is usually a white powder which is sniffed or eaten. Much more rarely it is injected. Cocaine is, and has always been, very expensive in this country. Definitely an up-market drug.
What does it do?	It is a fashionable stimulant. It makes you feel excited, inebriated. It can make you feel nightmarish. It can speed up thoughts to the point of *temporary* insanity. It gives temporary confidence.
Dangers	Cocaine can produce extreme fear of imaginary threats and aggressive anti-social behaviour. Cocaine is addictive and destructive to body tissue. Withdrawal, without treatment, can lead to psychiatric disorders. A regular long-term user *will* suffer mentally and physically.

Action recommended	Immediate help would include protection from rash actions and an attempt to calm the client. A long-term strategy to prevent further use is definitely called for but very difficult to devise. Seek medical advice.

Opiates—opium, morphine, codeine, heroin

This group of drugs is based on the ancient drug opium and represents the biggest business on the black market.

All these drugs are physically addictive. That is to say that the body adjusts to them so that when someone stops taking them the immediate effect is unpleasant and may even cause illness.

Opium

What is it?	It is a brown sticky substance, derived from opium poppies, which has to be carefully prepared so that it can be either smoked or drunk like tea. Not common in crude form in England.
What does it do?	The first effect is nausea. It then makes you dream, see visions. Large doses produce a particular kind of sleep. In Victorian times it was mixed with alcohol to produce laudanum. Coleridge, William Wilkie Collins and De Quincey were famous users. All suffered terribly from their addiction.
Dangers	Sleeping users may become ill and drown in their own vomit. Many people have experimented with opium without lasting damage, but long-term users sink gradually into a deep lethargy and suffer from effects similar to premature ageing.
Action recommended	Opium is not likely to appeal, or be available, to many young people. Immediate help would include keeping a very deeply sleeping subject out of coma by trying to rouse him or her. For long-term help for habitual users seek medical advice.

Morphine
A clear liquid derived from opium. This synthetic opiate relaxes the muscles and dulls the nervous system to reduce pain. It therefore appeals to anxious people. **Pethadine** is a similar drug which is less nauseous. Morphine is usually injected.
Immediate help as for opium.

Heroin

What is it?	The world's most notorious drug is a synthetic opiate, usually in white powder form.
What does it do?	It is a powerful depressant, which means it depresses the metabolism and the nerves so that you feel as if you didn't have a care in the world. Unfortunately it takes its toll while it does this and when you come down you are likely to suffer from sickness, cramps and a variety of adverse emotional states.
Dangers	Heroin is usually injected. It is highly addictive. It is very expensive and people often have to deal in it in order to afford it. The people who trade in it on a massive scale are really not at all interested in anyone's well-being but their own. The fact that heroin is very difficult to give up forms the basis of their trade. The hazards for morphine and heroin are heightened by the hazards of injecting (of 'fixing'). Dirty needles can kill. Air in the blood can kill. Impurities in the heroin, transferred into the blood, can kill.
Action recommended	Immediate help as for opium. People regularly using opiates need continuing help *but* **a** they will not necessarily welcome it. **b** the cure rate for established users is low. **c** one addiction is often exchanged for another. Off heroin onto alcohol is very common. **d** regular users become part of a fraternity with its own language, its own ethos. The drug attracts insecure people who have

been unsuccessful in establishing a stable identity. Merely getting them off the drug will not cure this.
For habitual users seek medical advice.

Stimulants—pep-pills, amphetamines, speed

Benzedrine and methedrine

What are they?	These are the most commonly abused stimulants. They are still quite widely prescribed and are, therefore, easily obtainable. Most stimulants bought on the black market are pills. They come in many shapes and sizes. More rarely people buy powder (which is very often amphetamine sulphate) which is injected.
What do they do?	They speed up the metabolism and make stored energy suddenly available. You feel excited, energetic, strong, brave perhaps. You are liable to talk a lot and you have to keep moving. Holding a conversation with someone who is 'speeding' is an exhausting business. These drugs do not *give* you energy. They make you burn up your reserves. Afterwards you feel terrible because you have all the symptoms of exhaustion, mentally and physically.
Dangers	This group of drugs has been popular among young people for a long time now and it is relatively likely that you will encounter users. They are harmful for the following reasons: **a** Users require bigger and bigger doses to get the same effect. **b** They reduce appetite drastically—'speed freaks' are really thin. (It was once prescribed for slimmers.) **c** Insecure people get Dutch courage from the drugs and can become very dependent psychologically.

	d The come-down is very unpleasant and people naturally want to go back up quickly.
Action recommended	Immediate help is not often urgent. The user will whizz around and feel terrible afterwards. Keep people off food that is difficult to digest (like cheese)—the body cannot cope while 'speeding'. Long-term help is needed for very regular users because they will tend to be undernourished, somewhat paranoid and prone to ulcers as a result of overactive muscles and glands. 'Speed' appeals to aggressive cults (football rowdies) in the same way as alcohol. Expect aggression (not necessarily physical) when trying to interrupt its use.

Depressants

Barbiturates—sedatives, sleeping pills, tranquillizers, downers

What are they?	The most widely prescribed group of drugs and always available on the black market in some form. Mostly these drugs come in pills; sometimes in liquid form.
What do they do?	Some put you to sleep, some just make you feel comfortably drowsy. For the illicit user the trick is to take the overdose that leaves him or her awake to enjoy it—a rather bizarre business akin to heavy gin drinking. The symptoms are very similar to drunkenness.
Dangers	Large overdoses of these drugs can kill. They switch everything off completely. In fact one of the commonest methods of suicide is the barbiturate overdose. But millions of people use these drugs and many abuse them in the sense of not sticking to the prescribed doses. The result is an addiction which is not always obvious to the outsider.

Action recommended	Immediate help includes keeping people off alcohol—the mixture is very dangerous. Keep people awake if possible. If people do pass out get help fast. Long-term help needs to focus on the mental state of the person. Motives are connected with a determined urge towards escapism which goes beyond mere fancifulness. Regular users of barbiturates could very easily be attracted to opiates.

Hallucinogens—psychedelics

LSD (acid), mescalin, psylocibin

What are they?	These drugs are not widely used in medicine and never prescribed. They are manufactured specially for the black market. They have been highly controversial for three decades. LSD (acid) is the one people will get hold of. It is colourless and tasteless. The most common form is tablets. These may contain other chemicals or impurities because they are not made in pharmacies. The amounts of LSD needed for a 'trip' are minute and the tablets are therefore tiny.
What do they do?	The effects of these drugs vary enormously from person to person because they work on the mind. Most people notice that their senses are greatly enhanced. Simple things take on the magnificent significance which they had on first encounter in childhood. Thoughts entering the mind are enlarged and embellished into intricate, sometimes beautiful, fantasies. Concentration is possible and problem solving may even be enhanced.
Dangers	There is no known overdose. No physical effects, either positive or negative, have been detected. The main hazard stems from the ways in which the drug accentuates what is already in the mind of the user. This means

that worries, fears, doubts, and obsessions can be greatly magnified. Nightmare mental crises can arise.

This drug is illegal and penalties can be severe.

Long-term users are altering their thought processes and social orientation radically. Psychedelic drugs may not be physically addictive but they are mentally seductive and there is no doubt that heavy use has precipitated many mental breakdowns.

Action recommended	Immediate help is not always needed. People are capable of wandering with child-like awe and excitement through the five to eight hours of an average trip. Sometimes the trip becomes overwhelming and the person becomes disorientated or emotionally distressed. In this case it is possible to distract the victim through some powerful or interesting sensory stimulus. Keep words simple and instructions clear. The aim is to enable the person to focus, to get things back in proportion. Be positive and light. Your attitude will be disproportionately interpreted by your client and if you are not careful you may be the agent by which a minor distress is translated into a major emotional or mental crisis.

Cannabis—dope—pot—hash—grass

What is it?	It is a weed which grows in many parts of the world. It has a 4000-year-old medicinal history although it is not now commonly used in medicine. It comes in many forms. All parts of the plant are toxic: roots, stems, leaves, flowers, and seeds are all used. The common forms are leaves and resin blocks. It can either be smoked or eaten.
What does it do?	First-time users often experience very little. It can make you feel relaxed, happy, interested in sensory stimuli, hilarious, and drowsy. In

DEIDRE POINTED OUT HER SUPPLY OF HASHISH FOR THE AUTUMN TERM

some respects it is like LSD in that the mental state of the user will very much determine the kind of experience generated. The physical effects do not seem to be very powerful and despite massive research there is no overall agreement on what they are.

Dangers

There is no known overdose. Millions of regular users throughout the world seem able to pursue satisfactory lives. The drug appeals to a very wide range of personalities and will not necessarily change the basic life-stance of the user.

Long-term effects are a controversial medical subject. There are eminent specialists who are prepared to align themselves publicly with both sides of the debate over whether the drug is harmless or harmful. There is some evidence that the active ingredients are cumulative in the body. In many cases the

	drug does seem to undermine concentration and prolonged use seems to affect memory. Some governments are now convinced that the drug's effects are overrated and that it is sufficiently harmless (some would say useless) to be left to individual discretion. In England it is illegal and the trafficking required to distribute it is punishable by heavy sentences.
Action recommended	Immediate help is not often needed. People may behave eccentrically but rarely completely out of character. In general the same approach as for LSD and the other psychedelics applies. Help the person keep a grip of reality and a sense of proportion.

Solvents (glue)

What are they?

The substances referred to are known as 'volatile solvents' because they become gases at room temperature and pressure. They are used where rapid drying is essential: they just evaporate away. It is not difficult, therefore, to get a quick idea of the kind of products containing them. The products include glues, paints, paint-strippers, nail varnish (and remover), lighter and cleaning fluids, spray cans and a great many other ordinary household products available at any hardware store, garage, or supermarket.

Occasionally the product will list its ingredients, but not always. The following are volatile solvents:

acetates (acetone), e.g. in paints; toluene, benzene, hexane, naptha (e.g. in moth-balls, air deodorants); trichloroethane (e.g. in typewriter erasers); ether, (e.g. in cleaning fluids); chloroform, amyl nitrate, nitrous oxide, freon (e.g. aerosol can gas); carbon tetrachloride (e.g. cleaning fluids).

What do they do?

They are similar in effect to alcohol (indeed, many are forms of alcohol). They progressively shut down the nervous system and relax inhibitions. Symptoms vary from person to person and depend on the exact product abused. In general they are similar to the signs of drunkenness and include:

slurred speech
lack of balance
uninhibited gestures
disorientation
silliness

Unlike drunkenness, running eyes and noses are common because these substances are irritants. Heavy intake can cause nausea and vomiting. A heavy user may become unconscious.

Regular users cannot easily disguise the powerful smell of the solvents and are also liable to have red marks around the mouth and eyes. Mouth ulcers are not uncommon.

N.B. Don't assume everybody with these signs has been sniffing glue!

Dangers

Inhaling is by far the most common method of abuse. Volatile solvents disperse in air, so people try to contain them in airtight containers, such as polythene bags and seal them around the mouth and nose in order to breathe the gases direct into the lungs undiluted.

Many young people will dabble with solvents with only temporary and slight damage to health. It is important to note, however, that there have been a number of serious first-time casualties; it is also significant that a number of the substances have a habit-forming potential.

Users are exposing themselves to the immediate risks of:

suffocation; eye damage from external contamination; the consequences of foolhardy acts performed while their judgement is impaired; lead poisoning in cases where lead-based paints and petrol are inhaled; asphyxiation from the use of aerosols.

There is a risk of heart failure from shock to the system due to very rapid intake of high levels of solvent. This risk has led to a comparatively small but significant number of fatalities.

Long-term effects have not yet been conclusively established. It is known that the liver and lungs are most vulnerable to solvent abuse. Non-lead paints contain hydrocarbons to which the body can develop a tolerance which can cause ill health. Toluene-based glues also set up tolerance and may lead to anaemia.

Action recommended

Act as for cases of drunkenness (see pp. 70–3).
Prevent self-destructive acts.
Isolate disruptive behaviour.
Confiscate source(s) of intoxication.
Get medical help if individual passes out, vomits, or complains of extreme discomfort.

Postscript

Some solvents have been available and used for fun since Victorian times when glue-sniffing, ether parties, and laughing gas demonstrations were not uncommon. By 1960 adolescent glue-sniffing had become newsworthy in England, but young people are by no means the only abusers of solvents. The present situation should not be allowed to get out of perspective.

Alcohol

What is it?

Alcohol is a depressant which slows down the functions of the nervous system. It is easily absorbed into the blood stream without having to be digested. The higher the concentration, the quicker it is absorbed. The proof percentage on beverages indicates the concentration of alcohol.

What does it do?

Alcohol has some effect on all the main body systems and many of the vital organs. In the stomach it activates the flow of digestive juices. Since alcohol does not, itself, require the action of these juices they have nothing on which to act, and they irritate the stomach lining. In the kidneys, alcohol inhibits the flow of a hormone which regulates the amount of urine produced by the body. The result is that too much urine is produced: hence one of the most obvious effects of drinking alcoholic beverages (often wrongly attributed to the quantity of liquid intake).

In the liver, one of the most complex and sensitive organs of the body, alcohol has a number of effects, the most serious of which is to block the function which balances the concentration of sugar in the blood. The brain is attacked directly by the alcohol as is the central nervous system. As more alcohol enters the blood the body's functions slow down progressively until the person lapses into a coma.

Dangers

The short-term dangers from drinking alcohol are well known. The highest risk for young drinkers is from road traffic accidents due to impairment of judgement and/or physical coordination. Alcohol is particularly dangerous when mixed with other depressants such as painkillers, sleeping tablets or tranquillizers. Rapid intake of alcohol after physical exertion can cause a 'heart attack'.

Long-term physical damage from habitual excessive drinking is most likely to occur in the liver and kidneys. The body will also attempt to adjust to regular intake of alcohol, spending more and more energy on dealing with it to the detriment of other bodily processes. One of the results of this is an increase in tolerance so that more and more alcohol has to be drunk to produce the desired inebriation. Another result is disorders of the major body systems especially digestion and breathing.

Problems

Because drinking alcoholic beverages is such an integral part of our culture, our attitude to problems arising from alcoholic poisoning are quite different from our attitudes to other kinds of poisoning or drug abuse. Young people have the additional problem that access to and tolerance of alcohol has become a rite of passage into adulthood.

Most young people drink occasionally and do so moderately. Their main motives are sociability and the need to feel accepted. Occasional excesses, for celebratory reasons, may create immediate risks but will not, in themselves, lead to long-term problems. Unless adults change the whole social attitude to drinking, young people will continue to feel a strong need to learn how to drink rather than how to abstain.

There is no doubt that some young people, like their elders, do use alcohol to mask or ameliorate problems. Depression, anxiety, loneliness, boredom, disappointment, and feelings of inferiority may lead a young person to seek solace in the effects of alcohol. Although alcohol does nothing to help the problems it is a fairly effective way of making some of them seem temporarily less painful. Because it is legal, acceptable, and readily available, alcohol is likely to remain a common resort for unhappy people.

Alcoholism is an illness which afflicts very large numbers of people in this country. It is currently classified as an actual disease although there is lively medical debate about the usefulness of this classification. The true dimensions of alcoholism can never be stated since precise definitions are not available and because many people with drink problems find ingenious ways of disguising their condition. They are also predominately unwilling to seek help. Indeed because regular heavy drinking is such an accepted feature of our society many people who would instantly admit they had a problem if they were compulsive users of almost any other drug, do not even realize that they are addicted to alcohol. The number of confirmed alcoholics under the age of 20 is relatively small but the foundations of alcoholism are most commonly laid during young adulthood.

Action recommended

The checklists in this section for dealing with all kinds of drug abuse apply to alcohol. From the point of view of first aid and immediate counselling and advice there is no particular distinction to be made between alcohol and any other drug. If alcohol has been mixed with other depressants, medical attention is advisable. Vomiting may alleviate nausea but it will have little or no impact on the level of inebriation. Alcohol is absorbed very rapidly and does not lie in the digestive system for very long. Certainly by the time someone feels sick most of the alcohol will have been absorbed. There is therefore little point in inducing vomiting.

It is also important to note that there is no readily available substance which can be given to a drunk to counteract the effects of the alcohol. Pills, medicines, and home cures are likely to be either dangerous or useless and should not be given.

A hangover is the body's way of complaining about the effects of blood sugar starvation. It will not be long before the body replenishes the level of blood sugar and no particular action is required. To some extent vitamin C and easily digestible sugar such as glucose speed up recovery.

Further help

It is helpful to adopt a skills approach to education and counselling about alcohol rather than a moral one. It is possible to use alcohol responsibly and young people want and need to learn how to do so. They need to know when, where, and how it is safe and sensible for them to drink. They need to learn to resist social pressures to drink. They need to be able to spot the signs that they are forming a drinking habit and know how to re-establish control of their drinking. The possession of skills like these are infinitely more use to a young person than a sense of guilt.

A major contribution to establishing a healthy attitude to drinking among young adults would be to change the image of the non-drinker. Drinking and even drunkenness are seen as tough or mature. Abstention is seen as weak and immature. There is much that educators could do to change these inaccurate and harmful images.

In order to help young people to learn how to use alcohol responsibly you will, of course, have to set a good example. You will need to have examined your own use of alcohol and your attitudes to the way others use it. Alcohol is so much part of our everyday lives that we tend to forget that we even have attitudes to it. These attitudes are apparent to others, however, and need to be clarified before you can respond helpfully to problems or questions about drinking.

Helping a young person cope with an alcoholic parent or guardian

A significant number of young people are themselves alcoholics and need help, but a very much larger number of young people are suffering from a whole range of problems arising from having an alcoholic parent. These people need help too but they are not necessarily going to ask for it directly because of the social stigma attached to alcoholism. They may feel that they are betraying the alcoholic parent by revealing his or her condition. They are very likely to feel confused and frightened by their situation. Any help you are able to give should be given against the background of the following considerations:

1. It is responsible for someone who is living with an alcoholic to seek help. It is not a betrayal and need not result in disgrace. Establish the fact that you, at least, are prepared to listen without blaming or breaking confidence.
2. The parent's alcoholism is not the young person's fault. Many children and young adults feel somehow that they are to blame for their parents drink problem. They may even have been told that this is so. Somehow you have to help the young person shake off this feeling.
3. The young person with an alcoholic parent is by no means alone. Alcoholism is fairly common. A statement of this fact may come as a great relief to some young people.

4 Alcoholism is an illness. People do not choose to live a life dependent on drink with all its unpleasant repercussions. To assert that alcoholism is an illness may enable a young person to cope with feelings of rejection by the behaviour of an alcoholic parent. It may be possible for him or her to see the parent as a person distinct from the alcoholism.

5 Alcoholics can recover. Young people may feel that the situation is hopeless and that there is no point seeking to remedy it. If hope is rekindled this may encourage the young person to seek help for the parent and in the process to gain help for him or herself.

6 Do not assume that there is no point in helping the child if the alcoholic parent is not receiving help. The young person needs all the help available to cope with the problems of living with an alcoholic. This means having someone to talk to about it, somewhere to go to escape from dangers resulting from it, and help in creating a personal lifestyle which is as unashamed, loving, and happy as possible despite the distressing behaviour of the parent.

6 First aid

The advice in this section is confined to:

1 The basic checklist of immediate aid which applies for all accidents and self-harming episodes.

2 A few special considerations about poisoning by drugs.

Basic life-saving checklist

On discovering an injured person, stay as calm, efficient, and observant as possible and follow the following sequence of procedures:

1 Protect the casualty from *immediate* danger.

2 Check whether the casualty is breathing. If, and only if, there is no sign of breathing, use artificial respiration.

3 Check whether the casualty is bleeding. Stop bleeding as quickly as possible.

4 Check whether the casualty is conscious. If the casualty is not conscious, prevent choking by lying in the recovery position.

5 Get help as quickly as possible.

More details about the life-saving checklist

1 **Protect the casualty from immediate danger.** It will usually be obvious if there is any **immediate** danger such as traffic, fire, caustic substances, etc. If it is possible to protect the casualty without moving him or her, do so. Only move the casualty if it is absolutely necessary to do so.

2 **Check whether the casualty is breathing.** Normal breathing is visible through movement of the chest. Faint breathing may not be very visible. Listen close to the casualty's mouth for the sound of breathing. Place a polished cold surface (e.g. spoon, mirror) close to the mouth of the casualty to check for signs of condensation from breath.

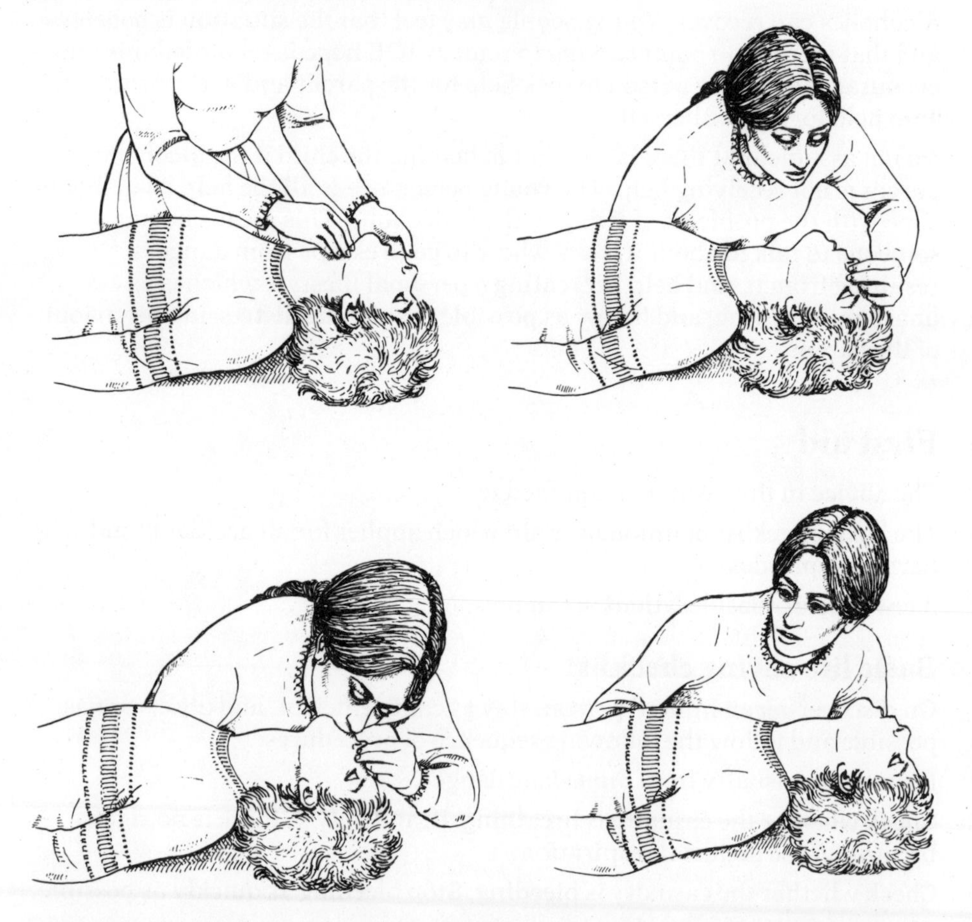

If, and only if, there is no sign of breathing, use artificial respiration. The most effective method is mouth-to-mouth respiration:

a Lie casualty on back.
b Clear casualty's mouth of debris, vomit, or any other matter.
c Tip chin up so that head is tilted back.
d Pinch nostrils to prevent air escaping from casualty's nose.
e Seal casualty's mouth with your own.
f Blow gently to inflate casualty's lungs with your own breath.
g Look to see casualty's chest fall as breath is exhaled.
h Repeat four or five times.

If the casualty is not breathing voluntarily after four or five artificial breaths, check the pulse on the side of neck. If there is no pulse, press down on the casualty's breast bone with one palm placed above the other. Do not allow your fingers to come into contact with the chest. Press down hard so that the chest is depressed 1½″. Allow the chest to rise again immediately. Repeat about 15 times. This will provide assistance to the casualty's heart and may start the pulse again.

Repeat artificial respiration and heart massage until breathing and pulse are operating voluntarily.

If the casualty vomits during this process, tip the head sideways to prevent choking.

It is dangerous to use mouth-to-mouth (or mouth-to-nose) artificial respiration on someone who is breathing normally.

3 **Check whether the casualty is bleeding.** Use your hands as well as your eyes. Blood is not always very visible either because of the position of the casualty or the colour or material of clothing. Stop any bleeding as quickly as possible. Most wounds will stop bleeding if they are sealed by pressure. Make a pad of the cleanest cloth you can find and press on to the wound. If you can press the edges of wound together do so. Bind the pad in place.

   It may be possible to remove loose debris from the wound but you should *never* attempt to remove objects which are embedded in the casualty. If necessary shape the pad to go round a protruding object and press the wound without driving the object further into the casualty.

4 **Check whether the casualty is conscious.** Ask questions clearly, fairly loudly, and repeatedly. Do not ask complicated questions. If you cannot obtain a coherent answer, assume that the casualty is not fully conscious. Many people die from choking or drowning in their own vomit or blood. Prevent choking by turning the person on to his or her front in the recovery position (sometimes called the 'three-quarters prone' or 'emergency' position).

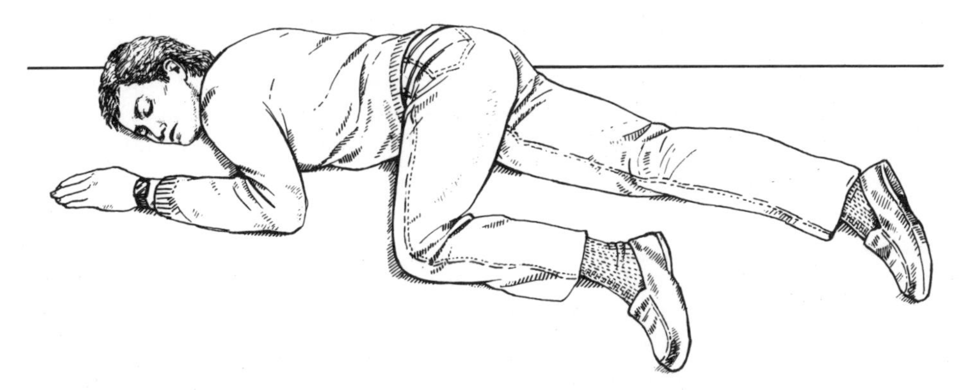

Loosen tight clothing at the neck, chest, and waist.
Check again for bleeding which may have been obscured when the casualty was lying on the injured part. Cover with something light and warm such a blanket or light coat.
Do not apply artificial heat such as hot water bottles.
Do not place anything under the head.

5 **Get help.** Do not leave the casualty longer than necessary. Call an ambulance unless it is obvious that the casualty can be safely delivered to a hospital quicker by some other means.
Give information to the emergency services clearly and slowly.
The most important items of information are which service—ambulance; and where you are—be prepared to give land marks as well as addresses or names.
Details of the casualty's condition are of secondary importance since ambulances are equipped to deal with a very wide range of contingencies.
Return to the casualty and watch his or her condition carefully. Repeat any of the above procedures if necessary. Otherwise do nothing except reassure the casualty and wait. Talk calmly and clearly; be attentive and uncomplicated. Concentrate on keeping the casualty as comfortable and free from distress as possible.

Self-inflicted injuries

These principles of first aid also apply for self-inflicted injuries. The most common results of self-harming episodes are bleeding, asphyxiation, and poisoning. The preceding notes are quite adequate for you to deal with bleeding however it has been caused. Slit wrists are a common form of self-harm which causes very extreme bleeding if the arteries are severed. Blood will pump out fast. Pad and bandage is still the best treatment although you may have to prevent the casualty from removing them.

The preceding notes are also quite adequate for you to deal with asphyxiation whether caused by hanging or gassing—the two most common causes. In the case of hanging, cut or untie the cord and keep it as evidence to show the police. In the case of gassing, make absolutely sure that you and the casualty are safe before proceeding with first aid. Turn off the source of gas. Open windows and doors and drag the casualty to a properly ventilated environment.

Poisoning by drugs

People who overdose in order to kill themselves or become a casualty needing attention are obviously aware that they are poisoning themselves. People who take drugs for kicks and injure themselves by overdoing the dose may not think of their action as self-poisoning. In either case they will not necessarily thank you for intervening and you may have to contend with uncooperative behaviour.

In the event of finding a person who is ill as the result of an overdose of drugs follow the procedures listed below. (In this context a person is ill if he or she has vomited, feels disorientated, is in pain, or has lapsed into unconsciousness.)

If the casualty is conscious:

1 Remove any remaining drugs, *but do not lose them or their containers*.

2 Find out *what* drugs have been taken;
how much has been taken;
when the drugs were taken.

3 If you have time, find out what the casualty knows about the normal dose, the purpose, and the effects of the drugs.
Do these things straight away in case the casualty lapses into unconsciousness. Information about the drugs may enable doctors to prevent permanent injury or death.

4 Seek medical help unless you have very reliable reasons for being certain that the casualty doesn't need it. Seek medical help if you have any doubt about:
the drug taken
the effects of the drugs taken
the amount taken
the effect of mixtures of drugs taken
the effect of the timing or method of taking the drugs.
Call the casualty's doctor or phone the emergency services and ask for an ambulance. Give any remaining (or suspected) drugs and containers to the doctor or ambulance officer.

If the casualty is unconscious:

1 Lie him or her in the recovery position.
2 Phone the emergency services and ask for an ambulance.
3 Keep samples of drugs (or suspected drugs) and their containers and give them to the ambulance officer.
4 Keep a close watch on the casualty.

In all cases of overdosing remember the following:

- Don't panic.
- Don't waste time with accusations, recriminations or other emotional reactions.
- Never administer any other substances even if you believe them to be antidotes.
- Take steps to prevent disorientated or suicidal persons from further harm.
- Be prepared to answer questions when help first arrives, at the hospital, and after the episode. There will almost certainly be some kind of follow-up enquiry.

Section C

Who else provides help for young people?

1 Health care services

The general practitioner

The GP is so familiar a figure that it may seem superfluous to describe the job. However, a number of changes are taking place in general practice which are of particular importance for young people:

1. Increasing interest in preventive medicine.
2. Increasing interest in the *social* aspects of health and disease.
3. Increasing recognition of the fact that the young person may not wish to be considered a member of a family in the same way as younger children are considered to be members.
4. Increasing numbers of women in general practice.
5. Growing interest in the beliefs that patients have about their own problems, the factors that cause their problems and influence their course.

Young doctors preparing for general practice now have a three-year training programme which involves both hospital work and supervised work in general practice. Many practices are 'training practices' and a trainee GP works with them. The aim of the training is to reorientate the GP from hospital medicine to community care.

GPs are not employed by health authorities. They are independent contractors who provide services for individual members of the public and are paid for these services by the Family Practitioner Committee which is a body that is independent of the health authority. An increasing number of GPs work as members of group practices and most GPs now work as members of primary care teams composed of GPs, district nurses, health visitors, and, occasionally, other professional staff.

Every young person is entitled to be on the list of a GP. To be put on the list of a GP when arriving in a new town the young person should find a GP who is said to be sympathetic to young people and see if the GP will accept him or her. Often the best GPs have so many people on their lists that they are not able to take any more. In such cases the young person can apply to the Family

Practitioner Committee to be put on a GP's list but of course he or she will not be able to choose the GP if this happens.

The young person who wishes to change from one GP to another is at liberty to do so. He or she simply has to find a GP willing to accept him or her and then to ask the receptionist, face-to-face or in writing, if the records can be transferred to the other GP.

Occasionally a GP may ask the Family Practitioner Committee to remove a patient from his or her list if it is obvious that the two cannot relate easily to one another. The Family Practitioner Committee is then responsible for appointing another GP.

The relationship between the GP and the young person has been much criticized. It has been said that the GP will be seen to be the family's agent but in practice this does not seem to be a major problem and as a result of the changes described in the opening paragraph, relationships between GPs and young people are probably improving across the country.

Because young people have so many fears about physical illness, although they have a low level of physical disease, the GP is an important person in the life of the young person and if a good relationship exists it should be a source of support for the young person.

GPs are wary of disclosing information to other people whom they do not know. The GP may ask for the written permission of the young person to be given before even discussing his or her problems.

However, an informal approach is usually best, either by writing to the GP outlining the topic you want to discuss or by phoning. When phoning it is appropriate to ask the receptionist when it would be convenient to speak to the GP and to give the name and date of birth of the young person so that the receptionist can look out the young person's records.

The health visitor

The health visitor is a fully qualified nurse who has studied midwifery and who has taken a full year's course in a polytechnic, usually after several years' work in hospital. Her main interest is in preventive medicine and in the health of the whole community, as opposed to the health of individuals. The health visitor will, however, be working with many individuals at any one time as well as taking an interest in her community.

Traditionally most of the work of the health visitor has been with mothers and very young children, but the pattern of work varies from one health visitor to another and there is increasing interest within health visiting in community work and in work with young people.

The health visitor is employed by the Health Authority. She works as a member of a team of nurses which usually covers a fairly large area. Usually the health visitor is linked with a small number of general practitioners: for example, there may be one health visitor working with a three-doctor practice and she is thus a member of the primary care team as well as a member of the team of nurses. In some parts of the country the health visitor has a specific geographical responsibility; in others her responsibility is seen to be to the 'community' who are on the list of the GPs with whom she works.

Health visitors have not in the past had much contact with young people except those who were parents. However, health visitors have increasingly been involved in family counselling, and thus often become involved when teenagers and parents are quarrelling; they are often involved in family planning work and they may be involved with young people at school as school nurses. In their work with families there is some overlap with the social worker.

Health visitors are particularly useful sources of advice on body maintenance—skin care, hair care, and problems of growth and development—and on specific problems such as cigarette smoking or alcohol abuse.

If you think that contact with a health visitor is appropriate the step to take is to phone the young person's general practitioner and ask the receptionist for the name and phone number of the health visitor who can be approached directly without involving the general practitioner; the health visitor works with a GP but not for him.

The school nurse

Sometimes the school nurse is a local health visitor but in secondary schools the person who is the school nurse usually does only school nursing, perhaps combining this with work in family planning clinics. She will have a close link with local health visitors and will be a member of the same team of community nurses as local health visitors; but the school nurse in such a position will be independent of the local health visitors and accountable to a nursing officer.

There is no nationally recognized system of training for school nurses. In many cases the school nurse will be a qualified health visitor. In most parts of the country Local Health Authorities will organize in-service training and induction training for nurses working in schools and there is a useful opportunity for people working with young people to meet together in such training courses.

Often the school nurse for a secondary school will also be the school nurse for a number of the feeder primary schools and may have a very good knowledge of families she has known for years.

Few secondary schools now have routine medical inspections of all pupils so there is no way in which the school nurse can have contact with all the children in the school. She is more likely to be involved with individuals and with groups with particular problems. Some school nurses run weight-watchers groups; others may have a group of children who wish to give up cigarette smoking; and yet others will be helping school children with physical disabilities. The school nurse may also be involved when a child is away from school frequently because of sickness.

The school nurse will also be helping school teachers with relevant parts of the curriculum, for example with parentcraft and home economics, and with health education.

The simplest way to get in touch with a school nurse is to phone the school office and ask either when the school nurse is next expected or for the phone number of the school nurse's central office, which will usually be the nursing office for the locality.

School doctors

Although medicine is dominated by two types of doctor—the hospital doctor and the general practitioner—there are other types of doctors in lesser numbers. One of these is the **clinical medical officer**. Clinical medical officers may have worked in hospitals or in general practice but now work in family planning clinics, child health clinics, or in school health: usually in a combination of two or three of these services.

In rural areas the school doctor may be a local general practitioner and this may also be the case with secondary schools; but in cities it is customary for clinical medical officers to be school doctors and to work closely with the school nurse in providing help and advice to the staff.

The work of the school doctor is concerned with the prevention of disease (principally through vaccination and immunization), with health education (by giving assistance to the health education officer who is the adviser to the school), and by giving advice to individual young people about their health problems and the impact their health problems have on their education. Handicapped children are the main focus of attention for the school doctor. The school doctor will, however, see many other young people at school, for example pupils who are frequently absent, giving as the excuse that they are ill; or pupils who are refusing to take physical exercise for reasons of ill health.

Usually only a small proportion of young people will know the school doctor although most will have had school contact at least once, when receiving a jab at an immunization session. Children with physical or psychological problems may be known to the school doctor but if the school doctor is happy that the school has all the information that it needs about a child's ill health and that the parents are not concerned about the effect of ill health on the child's schooling, then the school doctor may not wish to become involved with the young person who has adjusted well to health problems.

Family planning services

Every Local Health Authority in the National Health Service runs open-access clinics where advice and contraceptive supplies are free. The clinics also provide the quickest results of pregnancy tests—with an on-the-spot answer. Appointments can be made (clinics are listed under 'Family Planning' in the telephone directories) but no one is turned away even if no appointment has been made. Confidentiality is strictly observed.

The clinics are staffed by specially trained and experienced doctors and nurses; they alone see the clinical notes. The clinic receptionists welcome those who attend, answer the phone, give out supplies, and make appointments. Some clinics train doctors and nurses at some of their sessions but a patient can always be seen on her or his own if she or he so requests.

Family doctors have given a free family planning service since 1975. Patients can be seen by their own GP or any other doctor who is willing to give family planning advice. In the Family Practitioner list, available at main post offices or public libraries, doctors are marked C⋆ if they will give family planning advice to their own patients only, and C if they will see anyone.

Young people of any age are welcome at any family planning clinic, but there are Young People's Advisory Clinics specially for them. It is responsible for young people to seek contraception if they are sexually active. They have particular need of a counselling approach in the giving of contraceptive advice, taking into account the pattern and quality of relationships within their own family, and exploring their anxieties about themselves and others. This is the approach which a Young People's Advisory Clinic will take. Young people can be seen individually or with friends (of either sex). Adults with pastoral responsibility for young people find it very helpful to get to know one or more of their local family planning doctors. They are welcome to visit clinics for information or to introduce young people who have asked for help.

Health Education Units

Health Education Units are staffed by one or more **health education officers** and a varied number of support staff, including administrative, clerical, technical, or graphical staff. They are usually funded by the National Health Service at District Health Authority level and are responsible for developing health education with a geographical area. Each Unit has its own level of resources, and works according to its individual policy. Their aim is to improve public awareness of the means by which illness can be prevented; knowledge about health services (and how to make the best use of them); and awareness of the social factors that cause ill health.

The main interests of the Health Education Unit will vary from one part of the country to another but almost all Health Education Units spend a significant part of their time working with schools and increasingly with Colleges of Further Education and the Youth Service. It is recognized that health is affected by attitudes, values, and patterns of behaviour learnt as part of the continuous process of socialization. Educators are expected to take part in this process and realize the expectations of parents, the government, peer professionals, public service bodies such as the National Health Service, industry, and pupils. These expectations are usually conflicting and rquire a high level of ability in developing appropriate learning activities. It is this ability which is one of the prime concerns of health education officers and their Units support educators in the following ways:

1. **Supplying information** on the content for health education programmes, recent research, curriculum development and educational methods. Also information about organizations that can supply speakers, or information, on health topics.
2. **Training** in educational methods appropriate for health education, either through in-service courses or work with individual educators; also advice on courses for professional development in health education.
3. **Promotion** of small-scale initiatives in schools, colleges, and youth groups by advisory services and limited funding.
4. **Curriculum development**, especially aiming to encourage schools and colleges to integrate health education within the general curriculum.
5. **Providing learning aids**; most Units can offer a stock of resources such as leaflets, posters, films, and books on topics related to physical, social, and mental well-being. It is, however, inappropriate to expect the Health Education Unit to provide help at short notice and the best time to consult the unit is when the curriculum is being designed and not when the session is imminent.

If you do not know the telephone number of your local Health Education Unit, telephone the headquarters of the Local Health Authority.

2 Social support and supervision services

Social workers

Social workers are employed by the Social Services departments of local authorities. They are the professionals through whom local governments fulfil statutory obligations to provide a wide range of services for the welfare of their citizens. The main recipients of these services are the elderly, children and families in need or difficulties, physically and mentally handicapped persons, and disabled persons.

Social workers must have qualified for a Certificate of Qualified Social Work. Training is in the full range of social work services even though workers may subsequently specialize. There are various further training courses for specialists.

There are several basic types of social work but the two most common are social casework and residential social work.

Social caseworkers work with individuals or families to tackle specific problems. They have to assess the problem through interviews and various investigations and devise strategies for improving matters or removing the problem altogether. If they are unable to tackle the problem themselves, caseworkers are responsible for referring the case to those who can. They are therefore frequently liaising with health service workers, the legal professions, the Department of Health and Social Security, and so on. Generic (general purpose) caseworkers usually work in area teams covering a defined locality.

Some caseworkers are specialists. The specializations which are most relevant to the welfare of young people are psychiatric social workers (described in the section 'Psychiatric and welfare services', p. 95), and the medical social workers who are attached to hospitals, clinics, and out-patient centres. Medical social workers are concerned with the rehabilitation of those who have been ill and are returning to normal community life. They also have investigative and supportive roles as part of medical teams which may also include physiotherapists, speech therapists, and paediatricians.

Residential social workers provide continuing care through hostels, homes, and in some cases residency in private houses to care for individuals. Their main work with young people is in institutions which provide residential care for children in the legal care of the local authority. (A full description of the range of situations which give rise to an order for such statutory care is given on p. 101.) Residential social workers rely on the support of a number of different types of paid and voluntary workers who help to run the homes and hostels. Not all of these support staff are trained.

Individuals and families may approach their local Social Services department direct for help and the chances are that among the young people in your care are several whose families are receiving help as a result of direct approaches of this kind. They may have had material difficulties such as homelessness, poor housing, or poverty, or they may have more complex problems such as worries about the emotional welfare of one of the family members, runaways (children under 16 leaving home without permission), or a break-up of the family unit.

The other ways in which social workers become involved with their clients is through court orders. Since the court orders linking young people to social workers overlap with those which involve the Probation Service they have been dealt with together in a later section (see p. 87).

Social workers welcome, and sometimes rely on, the cooperation of teachers and youthworkers. It is useful for any school, college, or youth group to have some channel of communication to a Social Services department. In some neighbourhoods educators and social workers meet regularly to coordinate plans for the welfare of young people in the locality. Teachers are also likely to become involved in case conferences where a panel of social workers (and sometimes health care workers) have to decide how best to help an individual in the light of the information at their disposal. Knowledge of a young person through contact at school over a period of time has frequently proved invaluable at case conferences. You may also find that social workers can supply you with information which explains, or gives a context to, puzzling behaviour on the part of young people. Bear in mind, however, that social workers have to respect confidentiality.

Contact social workers through your local Social Services department, or in the case of specialists, through the unit to which they are attached.

Probation officers

In England and Wales probation officers work for national Probation Services. These are administered through committees of magistrates and judges which cover areas which are nearly all coterminus with county boundaries. Funding for the Service is mainly through the Home Office, but local authorities contribute approximately 20% at present. In Scotland probation and after-care is the responsibility of the social work department of the local authorities and a similar range of services is provided through specialist social workers.

Probation officers perform a range of duties arising from the work of civil and criminal courts. These duties can be grouped into two main areas of work; the preparation of reports for courts and penal institutions; and the supervision of offenders. The main duties of probation officers in relation to young people are described in a later section of this book (pp. 86–8). Several of these duties are shared, or overlap, with those of social workers; the two are therefore described together.

Probation officers work in teams which are assigned to court divisions. Some probation officers are specialists. The main specializations relating to young people are community service and hostel management. The duties arising from these specialist functions are described elsewhere. Probation officers are increasingly involved in day-care programmes aimed to prevent offenders from getting into further trouble. These include drop-in centres, educational and training programmes for those with very poor employment prospects, and drug and alcohol centres. These programmes are nearly always run in partnership with other professionals such as health care workers, social workers, and youth-workers.

Probation officers have the difficult task of giving personal support to individuals with whom they become closely acquainted, and satisfying the demands of the punitive systems of society. They are expected to make 'objective' assessments of the character of individuals who have yet to be tried in courts, befriend those who are serving sentences, and care for those who have served their sentences and are re-entering the community. In recent years they have had considerable influence on the growth of alternatives to custodial sentences.

Contact probation officers through your local Probation and After-care Service Offices, or through the specialist units to which they are attached. In Scotland contact the specialist social workers involved in probation schemes through the social work department of the local authority.

Probation officers and social workers in relation to criminal proceedings

This section deals with the work done by probation officers and social workers arising from legal matters affecting young people. It should be read in conjunction with the legal summaries in this book (pp. 98–108).

It is the Government's intention that Social Services departments will eventually take over all the work arising out of the juvenile courts. For various reasons this has been difficult to implement and the current situation is that a few local authorities have divided the work-load in this way, but the majority operate a mixed system with probation officers still supervising some people under 17. In all cases people over 17 are the responsibility of the Probation Service alone.

The work done by the two services in relation to the courts falls roughly into two categories: the preparation of social background reports and the supervision of offenders. The Probation Service also provides an after-care service for offenders who have been released from various forms of custody.

Social background reports (Social Services and Probation Service)

In most cases young people who are to be brought to court are interviewed at home or in an office in the Social Services or Probation Service (in the company of parents or guardians). Sometimes the nature of the offence, the previous record of the offender, or the family situation will lead to the young person being held in a secure assessment centre and interviewed there. The reports can draw on contributions from any adult who has intimate knowledge of the young person and will nearly always include a statement from the school of a school-aged child. It is up to the school to decide who should prepare a statement and usual for class teachers to be approached to contribute. Since the sentence passed by a juvenile court will be strongly influenced by the report such contributions are extremely important. Social background reports are always required for juvenile courts but courts dealing with people over 17 can decide whether or not to call for such reports.

Supervision (Social Services and Probation Service)

In the legal summaries you will see the full range of sentences which courts can pass. Supervision orders, attendance centre orders, or intermediate treatment orders involve the offender attending for regular interviews with a supervisor from one of the two services.

The effectiveness of such orders obviously depends on the relationship which the young person and the supervisor are able to develop. Frequently these relationships are strong and helpful, providing the support and guidance needed for people to establish themselves as responsible members of society. Some supervisors invite people to attend occasionally in the company of siblings or friends. Some Social Services departments and some probation offices run small-group sessions and drop-in facilities to provide support between interviews.

The duration of a supervision order is always specified but can be increased by a court if a subsequent offence is committed, or following failure to attend regularly. It is also possible for supervisors to return their clients to court to report the inefficacy of the order and recommending a change of sentence.

After-care (Probation Service)

Care and support may be given by various agencies to people who have been released from custodial sentences but the statutory obligation to provide it rests with the Probation Service. This includes young people leaving borstals and detention centres for whom the Probation Service provide an after-care service for at least one year following discharge.

There is a wide variety of methods by which probation officers provide after-care, ranging from regular formal interviewing to intensive rehabilitation programmes. Hostel accommodation with resident supervisors is available in some areas as are sheltered employment networks coordinated by the Service.

Probation officers and social workers in relation to non-criminal proceedings

There are many legal proceedings which affect young people and it is not the intention to give a full picture here. Social workers and probation officers are very heavily involved in the welfare of young people in relation to care orders, divorce and adoption.

Care orders (Social Services)

As indicated elsewhere, local authorities have responsibility for young people under 16 who are without adequate support or who require care and protection. It is possible for a local authority to obtain a court order (care order) which puts the young person directly in their care. They can make arrangements for guardians to look after young people or they can place them in homes run by the authority. Even if the young people remain at home it is possible for local authorities to obtain legal access to them to check on their welfare and offer counselling and guidance. It is the Social

Services departments, through their specialist caseworkers, who administer care orders.

Divorce (Probation Service; divorce court welfare officers)

Divorce courts and magistrates courts hearing matrimonial disputes have to be satisfied as to the arrangements for all children involved before granting a legal termination of marriage—a 'decree absolute'. To judge this they rely heavily on background reports prepared by probation officers (or special welfare officers attached to some divorce courts). Children are not legally able to contribute to divorce hearings directly so that the only way their interests can be established is by the testimony of their parents and the social background report. Probation officers take considerable trouble to ensure that they have discovered the state of allegiances in a family, and the material circumstances, in the hope that the court can discern the best possible arrangements for the welfare of the children.

Adoption (Social Services)

The aims and preconditions for adoption are set out in the legal summaries. Local authorities have responsibility, through their Social Services departments, for providing emergency accommodation for pregnant women and inadequately housed mothers with babies; assessing the needs of children being offered for adoption; vetting prospective adopters; and counselling people with problems relating to adoption.

General

Social workers and probation officers will welcome cooperation from other professionals who are caring for their young clients. Some of the schedules for social background reports make intensive investigations very difficult and information from teachers and youthworkers could be invaluable. It is possible for those attending courts with young people to ask for verbal testimonials from other professionals to be heard by the court and most courts will hear these. The case-load of social workers and probation officers is normally very heavy and they may not get to see their clients as often as they would wish. Offers from teachers and youthworkers to provide interim support for young people, if sensibly arranged, will often be welcome.

Juvenile bureau officers (sometimes known as Juvenile liaison officers)

Juvenile bureaux are a specialist section of police divisions. They consist of small teams of police officers to whom are referred all offences involving people under the age of 17 (legal juveniles). These officers may also participate in crime prevention programmes including school visits and links with youth organizations.

Juvenile bureaux employ varying procedures for dealing with juvenile crime but the aim is the same in all cases—to find an appropriate way of dealing with young offenders within a range of options, only one of which is to bring people to court.

A typical pattern of dealing with a young offender would be as follows:

The offence is brought to the attention of the local police; the case is referred to the local juvenile bureau; specialist officers arrange to interview the person(s) involved, usually at home and always with parents or guardians present. The officers also contact the Probation Office, Social Services, educational social workers and the head teacher of the relevant school (they will sometimes do this even if the person has left school). The officers may go further afield and seek information from other members of the family, youthworkers, employers, etc. The officers put together a report on the social background and character of the person(s) which may include conflicting opinions; the report is given to the Police Superintendent who has responsibility for community liaison; the Superintendent then decides from the information available which of the following courses of action to take:

1 Do nothing.
2 Administer an official caution.
3 Bring the case to the juvenile court.

The Superintendent must treat all the people involved in each case the same.

A caution is a strictly formal warning given by the Superintendent, in the presence of parents, in which the full details of the offence are rehearsed, the consequences of further offences spelt out, and the disapproval of the Superintendent made quite clear. Such a caution can only be made if one or more of the following conditions pertains:

1 The offender(s) admit(s) the offence and the police are satisfied that there is sufficient proof to take the case to court.
2 The parents or guardians of the young offender and any victims agree to this method of dealing with the offender.
3 The juvenile bureau, after consultation with the LEA and Social Services, agree that this is an appropriate way of dealing with the offender.
4 All culprits involved in this particular offence are to be treated in the same way.

It is possible to draw to the attention of a juvenile bureau young people who have not yet committed a crime, but are thought to be at risk of so doing. This might be appropriate, for example, in the case of a young person who is known to be spending a lot of time with hardened offenders or who is staying out very late and is unwilling to account for his or her whereabouts. Such referrals raise all kinds of moral issues, but have probably prevented some young people from getting into serious trouble. In these cases juvenile bureau officers have no jurisdiction to act without the permission of parents, but with such permission they may interview and advise the young person. Occasionally this uncovers situations in which the young person is a victim and needs help. Often juvenile bureau officers are sufficiently familiar with the communities they serve to be able to act informally to stop young people drifting towards serious crime, although this role is more frequently undertaken by crime prevention and community policemen. In some metropolitan areas with very high incidences of juvenile crime there are sophisticated community policing networks to augment the basic juvenile bureau system described here.

Contact juvenile bureau officers through your local police station or indirectly through educational social workers (education welfare officers).

Intermediate treatment (IT) workers/officers

The responsibility for providing this service has come to rest with the Social Services departments of local authorities, most of whom employ at least one, and usually a small team of full-time professional IT officers. These full-time workers will nearly always recruit part-time or other professional helpers: probation officers, youthworkers, and voluntary workers in clubs, hostels, and centres, are frequently involved. Not all social workers with responsibility for IT are freed entirely from other duties.

Intermediate treatment is a way of helping young people who have been in trouble with the law. It bridges the gap between a custodial sentence and leaving the person in the community without supervision and guidance. As outlined elsewhere, courts can require young people under 17 to attend an IT group on a regular basis.

The actual programme developed by IT officers is not prescribed by the legislation and each local team is free to devise its own. The general idea is to keep the young person in the community but to create influences that counteract the factors in his or her personal life which have led him or her into trouble. To achieve this a wide variety of strategies have been employed which range from very informal recreational groups to planned behaviour modification. The latter usually involves a programme in which specific behaviour changes are set as targets along with incentives for achieving them.

Most IT involves a programme which starts with an assessment period in which the personality, circumstances, and interests of the young person are explored. A personal programme will then be arranged which will probably involve integrating the young person into a small IT group and later into ordinary community groups. Sometimes the young person is attached to a community group (youth club, art or sports centre), with supervision, from the outset. Individual counselling is nearly always available.

IT groups often engage in practical projects with a tangible end product. Expressive artistic and sporting activities have also proved to be useful vehicles for what is basically a social re-education programme.

It is of the essence of IT that it not only takes place in the community, but makes use of local people and institutions. The IT officer may be offering some of the young people with whom you are involved a carefully thought-out opportunity to improve the quality of their lives, and you, in turn, may be able to contribute to this programme. IT officers may be able to help young people whom you identify as being 'at risk' before they fall foul of the law, but they are not obliged to do so.

To contact IT officers apply to your local Social Services department.

3 Youth and community services

General aims and organization

Most youthwork is done by part-time workers but nearly all local authorities employ a certain number of full-time professional youthworkers. The actual department which controls youthwork varies: the most common is Education, but in some authorities the Recreation or Social Services departments take responsibility. As you will see below, the work done by youthworkers is extremely various, but most have in their contracts some reference to:

a the social education of young people;

b the provision of informal recreational and learning opportunities for young people.

It is quite common for counselling to form part of the job description.

Some types of full-time youthwork

Club leader A very large number of youthworkers are employed to run multi-purpose youth centres. Sometimes these are separate and purpose-built, but frequently they are attached to a school, college, or community centre. In these centres the leader will arrange a programme of evening sessions, recruit and supervise part-time helpers, and generally manage the building(s).

Area worker Some youthworkers are not employed to run specific clubs but have a supervisory role in relation to several clubs. An area worker would be expected to help with recruitment and training of workers for these clubs and would typically have a role in their management.

Detached youthworkers Once a small specialist band of pioneers, this aspect of youthwork has grown enormously in recent years. A detached worker may have connections with clubs or schools but does most of his or her work in places where young people spontaneously congregate such as cafés, street corners, pubs, and shops. Some detached projects are set up to deal with specific problems such as runaways, drugs, and teenage prostitution, but many projects are not problem-based and exist as a way of reaching young people who are not catered for by clubs and other institutions. Inevitably detached workers find themselves involved in counselling and in relating to some young people who are at odds with society.

Specialist youthworkers In many areas there are specialist youth centres with wardens or tutors in charge. Sports and Outdoor Pursuits Centres are common and Arts and Drama Centres are on the increase. The workers who run such centres obviously have to be experts in their field and will be involved in training adults and young people.

Note: The above categories are just a rough guide: Many workers have job descriptions which overlap these categories. For instance it is now common for club workers to be asked to undertake some detached work. Some workers have split appointments and may also be involved in adult education or teaching.

Training officers Youthwork training, now a highly sophisticated branch of education, is innovative in the fields of groupwork, counselling and informal education. There are a number of full-time degree-level training courses and some colleges of education also run option courses in youth and community work.

Most local authorities support their youthworkers with a full-time training officer. These organize local courses covering the range of work undertaken in the authority. Increasingly training officers are involved in programmes at a regional level. Many training courses are a meeting point for voluntary, part-time, and professional youthworkers.

What can youthworkers offer?

Youthworkers maintain contact with a significant number of young people outside institutional hours and after they have left school. They may see another side of the lives of young people and will certainly have a different relationship to them from those who are in authority or *in loco parentis*.

Youthworkers may be able to shed light on puzzling behaviour or distress displayed at school or college. They may know families and/or friends who attend different schools.

Youthworkers can sometimes provide continuity of adult contact for young people coming out of their formal schooling or off the Youth Training Scheme.

Detached youthworkers reach the parts of society other adults cannot reach. They are able to shed light on extreme social deviance and the fate of those who have slipped through the statutory nets. They may therefore have a perspective on emotive current issues like drug abuse, glue-sniffing, or sexual fashions.

There is no statutory base to any kind of youthwork. There are no duties which youthworkers *must* perform. They are therefore under no obligation to share information or collaborate with plans for particular individuals. Experience has shown, however, that links with various kinds of youthworker are invaluable for other professionals with responsibility for young people.

4 Psychiatric and welfare services

Educational psychologists

Educational psychologists work for Local Education Authorities as part of school psychological services. They have to be qualified in both psychology and teaching, and have at least two years practical teaching experience. They pursue their investigative work through direct contact with schools, as part of advisory teams, and through contact with parents, social workers, and doctors. They pursue treatment independently, and in concert with psychiatric social workers, consultant psychiatrists, and other specialist workers.

Educational psychologists are the schools' referral point for children of all ages with serious learning difficulties and psychological problems. For such children they have to devise plans for education and, if necessary, treatment. They may arrange remedial teaching withdrawal to special (including residential) units and schools. They may also arrange therapy. These arrangements will be made, as far as is possible, with the agreement and active cooperation of parents, and will be determined by the procedures required under the 1981 Education Act for Children with Special Educational Needs.

Each team of educational psychologists devises its own referral and follow-up strategy, but a typical pattern would involve the following stages. The young person is usually referred to the school psychological service by a school, although direct referrals from parents are possible. The psychologist concerned confers with teachers and arranges an interview with the young person and his or her parents. The nature of the suspected problem is explored and after this or subsequent interviews the psychologist prepares a report. This report is often shown to the parents and agreed with them. The report may be a summary of the involvement of the psychologists in a plan of action which may involve some simple extra help at school or strategies of varying complexity, through to a complete programme of special education or therapy. If therapy is agreed the parents may well be asked to attend some or all of the sessions. The educational psychologist may be involved in treatment as a counsellor, as a family therapist, or as a co-therapist working alongside psychiatric social workers and consultant psychiatrists.

Educational psychologists are responsible, with others, for keeping under review all students who are receiving special education and treatment, whether they are attending ordinary schools or special units. They also act as advisers for the Local Education Authority on policies for special education and can be influential in shaping approaches to ordinary classroom practice. They are frequently contributors to the in-service training of teachers, especially in relation to strategies for assessing difficulties and coping with children with special needs.

Educational psychologists may try to see school students in their homes, schools, and other settings in order to understand them more fully. Thus they are frequently in regular contact with whole families and may welcome background information from other people with intimate knowledge of the family. On the other hand they have to be discreet, very conscious of confidentiality, and may feel unable to share information, or even to seek it, outside the family and school context.

Many educational psychologists are involved in offering advice and counselling to parents on child-rearing and the problems that can arise in families, even if there has been no official referral of a member of the family.

Contact educational psychologists through the local Education Offices.

Psychiatric social workers

Psychiatric social workers may be employed by Social Services, Health Services, or Local Education Authorities. In all cases they are part of a general provision of child guidance and work alongside educational psychologists and consultant psychiatrists.

It is difficult to generalize about the exact way in which psychiatric social workers operate. At one time a large number of psychiatric social workers were attached to Guild Guidance Clinics where they were responsible for taking referrals to the clinics and making investigations concerning these referrals. There has been a move away from Child Guidance Clinics and various alternative strategies have been tried. It is still usual, however, for psychiatric social workers to be involved in investigations about family background and social circumstances.

They will visit families at home or receive them in whatever centre has been set up for helping children with psychological problems. They may discuss with the parents the nature of the problems affecting their child and then prepare a preliminary assessment of the situation with as much background information about the whole family as possible. They may then arrange for the child and parents to attend an interview with a consultant psychiatrist. The whole child guidance team may then discuss the case and plan what kind of help is to be offered. Not infrequently a consultant psychiatrist will take responsibility for the main therapeutic programme with the child while the psychiatric social worker keeps in touch with the family. Sometimes psychiatric social workers are involved in the therapy arranged for young people and their families.

Psychiatric social workers provide one of the links between child guidance teams and the community. They process referrals from educational psychologists, educational social workers, schools, social workers, doctors, parents, and health visitors. They may also be involved in outreach projects to help the community understand the particular provision which is being made for the psychological care of young people in the locality. They will nearly always be involved in the training of health care and education staff with pastoral or therapeutic responsibilities for young people or their parents.

Contact psychiatric social workers through Child Guidance Clinics, where they exist, or through the local authority or health authority.

Educational social workers (sometimes known as educational welfare officers)

The role of the educational social worker (educational welfare officer) has developed away from its roots in the old attendance officers into a part of the general support service in most Local Education Authorities. Educational social workers are responsible through a Principal Educational Social

Worker to the Chief Education Officer and work closely with generic social workers, health visitors, probation officers and the juvenile liaison branch of police forces. They are usually required to be qualified social workers.

Educational social workers are concerned with the whole range of school children. They are responsible for assessing the problems which jeopardize the chances of a child benefiting from the educational opportunities offered by the Local Education Authority. They find themselves tackling a very wide range of problems including material deprivation, disruptive behaviour, mental or physical handicap, racial prejudice, persistent ill-health, and truancy.

Educational social workers are in the front line of contact with the parents and guardians of children. They help sort out practical difficulties which are preventing children from attending school as well as following up deliberate school truancy. They will try to solve truancy problems through talking to children and their families, but are empowered to start formal proceedings against parents if this approach fails.

Educational social workers find themselves mediating between families and schools. They also attend case conferences on young people, some of which they may convene themselves in order to bring together various people who share a concern for a particular young person. They have a key role in assessing the entitlement of families to free or subsidised services such as school meals, school uniform allowances, and transport to school.

The educational social worker is usually a familiar part of the community with links with all the main professions and institutions which affect young people. Many incidents or circumstances which might have an adverse long-term effect on young people can be ameliorated by reference to an educational social worker who can pick up the threads in time to prevent a serious situation developing.

Contact educational social workers through your local Education Office.

Consultant child and adolescent psychiatrists

Consultant child and adolescent psychiatrists are qualified medical practitioners who, having trained in general psychiatry, specialize in child psychiatry. They may be based in hospitals, usually in special units; or they may be based in the community, in clinics and Child Guidance Centres. In either case they are the leaders of multi-disciplinary teams which usually include educational psychologists, psychiatric social workers, clinical nursing staff, and, in some cases, child psychotherapists. Wherever they are based, child psychiatrists spend a considerable amount of their time in settings where disturbed young people are to be found. This involves them in direct contact with schools, colleges, children's homes, and foster homes, as well as family households.

The main responsibilities of child psychiatrists include the following:

1 The diagnosis and treatment of emotional and behavioural disorders in young people, including work with families as a whole group.
2 Providing consultancy for GPs, paediatricians, social workers, residential care workers, and educators with primary care responsibilities for young people.
3 Preparing legal reports for juvenile courts where there is concern about possible psychiatric disorders in young offenders.
4 Providing consultancy for in-patient services in hospitals.
5 Advising on measures and policies to promote the emotional well-being of young people and prevent disturbance. This involves considerable work with staff involved in residential care.
6 Training other psychiatric staff, including those described elsewhere in this section.

Although child psychiatrists are appointed by, and paid through, the National Health Service, they are not directly employed by the Service. They are free to pursue their own policies and practices within the broad guidelines of professional ethics. This enables them to devise and develop new strategies for diagnosing and treating behavioural and emotional disorders. For this reason the child and adolescent psychiatric hospital units and community based clinics vary considerably in their approaches.

It is in the nature of child psychiatry that it involves working with non-medical colleagues. Although educational psychologists are often the agents through whom referral from educators is conveyed to child psychiatrists, direct contact with teachers and youthworkers is quite common. Apart from having the final diagnostic responsibility for disturbed young people, child psychiatrists are a source of advice and training for educators in their primary care roles.

Contact consultant child and adolescent psychiatrists through Child Guidance Clinics or Child Psychiatric Units of hospitals. It is likely that most contact will be through previous referral to a GP, educational psychologist, or psychiatric social worker.

Section D

Background information on the law and young people

1 Criminal proceedings against children and young adults

The law separates people into three age groups for the purposes of trial and sentencing.

Children under 10 cannot be brought to trial. As discussed elsewhere however, courts have powers to arrange for their care and protection.

Children between the ages of 10 and 17 may be brought to trial. There are special juvenile courts to deal with offenders in this age range. These are presided over by magistrates who have been chosen for their special suitability for such work and at least one member of the bench must be a woman. The Press are allowed to attend but must not identify the defendant in any way. If the defendant is under 14 the onus is on the prosecution not only to prove guilt but to prove awareness of guilt, since children under this age are deemed to be unable to tell right from wrong.

Juvenile courts can:

1 Fine or order the convicted person to pay compensation. Naturally the parents of the child are obliged to meet these orders if the child is unable to do so.

2 Bind the child and/or his or her parents over to keep the peace for a specified period. If there is a transgression during this period the court can pass a more severe sentence.

3 Make a supervision order. This means that the child must attend for interview with a social worker or probation officer on a regular basis. The court may include in this order an intermediate treatment order. This would give power to the social worker to arrange for the convicted child a programme of activities which are felt to be beneficial in changing the behaviour of the child.

4 Make a care order.

5 Make an attendance centre order. This would require the child to attend, for a certain number of hours per week, a centre which provides a programme of remedial activities. This differs from intermediate treatment in that

attendance is at a prescribed centre, whereas intermediate treatment may involve integration into ordinary youth clubs, sports groups, etc. The minimum sentence is four months, the maximum twelve months. Young people up to the age of 21 may be required to attend these centres.

6 Send the child to a detention centre. (This applies to boys over 14 only; there are no detention centres for girls.) Sentence would be for a short time (less than a year) during which period the offender would be subjected to a very strict regime but with no emphasis on education in the normal sense.

7 Refer the case to a Crown Court with a recommendation for borstal training. This applies to young persons over 15. Borstal training entails a period of custody between six months and one year followed by a period of supervision in the community administered in the same way as a supervision order. Borstals are schools and provide a full programme of educational and recreational activities under strict discipline.

If the young person has committed a particularly serious crime, the juvenile court will pass the case to a Crown Court which may sentence the offender to long, or even indeterminate, periods of detention.

Young people over 17 years of age can be tried in an ordinary court and sentenced to the full range of adult sentences. The following are the main options open to the sentencer:

1 An absolute and conditional discharge. The offender is free provided he commits no offences during a prescribed period.

2 A suspended sentence. The court may suspend sentence for up to two years. If behaviour is good, a light sentence or absolute discharge may be passed. If an offence is committed during the period of suspension, the court may add to the sentence for the new offence an appropriate sentence for the original offence.

SHOPLIFTING

3 Imprisonment.

4 Probation. This is a supervision order for those over 17. The Probation Service administers the order. There may be a requirement to reside in a probation hostel (in the community) or to attend an attendance centre. Failure to comply can lead to a change of sentence or payment of a fine.

5 Community service order. This is an alternative to imprisonment, and would not normally be applied where the appropriate sentence was a fine. The offender is required to perform unpaid work in the community under lay supervision. The offender must consent to this order. The arrangements would be made by a probation officer. The order is made for a specified number of hours between 40 and 240. Failure to comply may lead to resentencing or a fine.

2 Non-criminal proceedings directly affecting children and young adults

Adoption

The purpose of adoption is to create a relationship with the adopters which offers all the rights and securities that child would have had if he or she had been their 'natural' offspring. Adoption orders transfer to the adopters all the responsibilities and liabilities of parenthood. Such orders supersede any temporary care orders which may have been made by the local authority. They are permanent and irrevocable except by further legislation.

To be eligible for adoption a person must be under 18 and unmarried.

To be eligible to adopt a person must be over 21 and resident in the British Isles. (In the case of a married couple this need only apply to one of the applicants.)

Children can only be placed for adoption by a registered adoption society, a local authority, or the parent or legal guardian.

The adoption order is made by a court of law when it is satisfied that the necessary agreements have been obtained. Agreement is normally required from every person who is a parent to the child. The agreement of natural fathers of illegitimate children is only required if they have custody of the child. A mother's agreement is only valid if it has been given in writing before a legal witness *after* the child has reached the age of six weeks.

The Court has the right to dispense with or override agreements if parents cannot be found, are unreasonably refusing, or if parents are not properly fulfilling their duties to the child and/or the child is at risk in their custody.

Children adopted before 12 November 1975 may ask to see their original birth certificates when they reach the age of 18, but they must first attend an interview with a counsellor provided by the local authority. A legal adult who was adopted after this date has automatic right of access to his or her birth certificate and may elect to have an interview with a counsellor.

Children in care

Local authorities have a statutory duty to care for children under the age of 17 if:

a they have lost or been abandoned by both parents and have no acting guardians.

b their parents or guardians are deemed to be unable properly to provide for them.

c their parents or guardians are treating them in such a way that the intervention of the local authority is deemed necessary for the welfare of the child.

The child may be taken into care under Section 2 of the Child Care Act 1980 on a temporary basis. If the circumstances change the child may be returned.

A child may be taken permanently into care under Section 3 of the same Act if there appears to be no hope of the natural parents or guardians assuming parental responsibilities. The law sets out a number of conditions for this judgement which include mental disorders and unsuitable lifestyles as well as the obvious contingency of death or desertion. Parents have the right of appeal against such orders to the High Court.

Children may come into the care of a local authority through the order of a court of law. Courts make such care orders if one or more of the following conditions are satisfied:

1. The child is being ill-treated, or his or her proper development is being avoidably impeded; or the child's health is being avoidably impaired or neglected.
2. There is reason to believe, through knowledge of another child who is or was a member of the same household, that the conditions in 1 will be satisfied.
3. A person who has been convicted of offences described in 1 above is, or may become, a member of the same household as the child.
4. The child is regarded as being in moral danger.
5. The child is regarded as being beyond the control of his or her parents or guardians.
6. The child is of compulsory school age and is not receiving efficient full-time education suitable to his or her age, ability, and aptitude.
7. The child is guilty of an offence other than homicide. (In the case of homicide the child will usually be placed in a secure Home Office establishment.)

The court can only make a care order if the child is unmarried and under 16 years of age.

Local authorities are required to investigate if there are reasonable grounds for suspecting that one of the above conditions is satisfied. Care proceedings may also be brought by a police officer or the NSPCC.

Care orders remain in force until the child reaches the age of 18 unless varied by a court of law.

Local authorities will normally care for their charges by boarding them out to suitable paid foster parents or placing them in community homes. Community homes are institutions run by the local authority under professional staff. In some cases these homes are 'secure', meaning locked and closely supervised with limited access to visitors.

3 Divorce

Since children are not parties to divorce actions they are at risk of being used as pawns in the official disputes of their parents. Even if they are not abused in this way, it is still likely that divorce will adversely affect them. The divorce laws have been revised recently to take more account of the plight of children but they are still clumsy and cannot protect children from emotional damage. Of course the divorce itself is only the official recognition of what may have been a long and miserable process of disintegration. It may even bring relief.

Marriages can be legally severed by divorce courts and magistrate's courts. Recent legislation has brought the powers of the two more into line. The most notable remaining difference is that the magistrate's court cannot dispose of property. At the very beginning of proceedings for divorce full statements have to be made about the children involved and the plans for their welfare. The court will begin by investigating grounds for divorce regardless of the welfare of the children but will only grant a full legal divorce—'decree absolute'—when satisfied that the best possible arrangements have been made for all the children involved; or that it is not practical for the parties in the divorce to make such arrangements. In the latter case the court can make immediate temporary arrangements for the care of the children and long-term arrangements such as a care order.

The court is concerned with all people under 16 or in full-time education who are the children of, or in the care of, the parties to divorce. The court can also decide that other people shall be considered as children for the purposes of the divorce proceedings (such as handicapped young people over the age of 16). It can hear applications relating to the children not only from the parties but from certain other persons: guardians of the children; people who have been given previous care and custody of the children by a court; the official solicitor; a local authority; or any other person to whom the court has given permission to apply for custody and/or maintenance of the children.

Helped by a report from a probation officer, on the circumstances of the children in the family, the court must decide upon the following matters relating to the welfare of the children:

Maintenance, i.e. who is going to have responsibility for ensuring that the children are kept in the financial position in which they would have been had the family remained intact?

Custody, i.e. who is going to be allowed to influence important decisions about such things as politics, religion, education, moral tenets, in relation to the child? In legal terms, custody does not imply that such a person is living with the children. The day-to-day influence on the children is referred to as **care and control** and is considered as a separate, but related, matter.

Access, i.e. who is going to be allowed to visit the children? Will this person be allowed to have them to stay? What strings will be attached to the right of access?

Matrimonial home, i.e. what is to be done about ownership or tenancy of the family home? In the past the home has been regarded by courts as simply another property to be disposed of equably between the two parties. This has frequently meant the sale of the home and the uprooting of the children. Recently courts have taken more account of the right of the children to influence decisions affecting where they are to live and have recognized their interest in continuity. Magistrate's courts, however, have no jurisdiction over property and can only influence this matter indirectly.

Protection from violence, i.e. do steps need to be taken to protect the children from existing or likely violence at the hands of either of their parents? Children are protected from violence by other legal acts but it is possible for divorce courts or magistrate's courts to interrupt proceedings and take immediate action to protect children, including the arrest of one or both parents. The full range of care orders can be invoked.

4 The law and the tenant

The two key Acts of Parliament are:

1 The **Rent Act** 1977

2 The **Housing Act** 1980

Rent

Who fixes the rent?
The landlord can fix the rent at any sum he or she wishes but any tenant has the right of appeal to a **Rent Tribunal** if he or she thinks the rent is fixed too high. The tribunal may decide to fix a lower rent and the sum it registers becomes the highest rent that can be charged for that property, unless the tribunal itself agrees to an increase. Under the 1972 Housing Finance Act, landlords and tenants can agree without recourse to a tribunal, but this does not interfere with the rights outlined above.

Who records rent payments?
If rent is paid on a weekly basis, a landlord must provide a **rent book** with the following items of information contained within it:

1 The landlord's name and address.

2 The amount of rent chargeable.
3 The tenant's rights under the rent laws.
4 The tenant's rights under local authority rent allowance schemes.
5 A statement of the maximum number of people who are legally allowed to dwell in the house.
6 An outline of the laws against overcrowding.

All weekly payments must be entered in this book.

Notice to quit

Fixed term tenancies are granted for a definite period of time after which they automatically end. When they end no notice to quit is necessary. However a tenant may have a statutory right to remain in tenancy under the Rent Act.

Periodic tenancies are those with no fixed end date. For these the landlord and the tenant are both obliged to give notice to quit.

Notice to quit: rules for the landlord

A valid notice to quite issued by a landlord must:

a be in writing.
b be given not less than four weeks before the end date which it mentions.
c terminate the tenancy at the end of a complete period of tenancy (e.g. the end of a month, if the tenancy is by the month).
d be longer than four weeks if the period of tenancy is longer than four weeks.

It must include mention of the following information:

1 If the tenant does not leave the dwelling, the landlord must obtain an order for possession from a court.
2 Such an order cannot be obtained before the notice to quit has expired.
3 A tenant who is not certain of his or her right to remain in possession, or is uncertain about any other aspect of his or her rights in the matter, can obtain advice from a solicitor. He or she may be entitled to legal aid. The tenant should also be able to obtain information from a Housing Aid Centre, a Citizens' Advice Bureau, a rent officer, or a Rent Tribunal Office.

Notice to quit: rules for the tenant

If a tenant wishes to give up the tenancy he or she must give notice to quit unless the landlord agrees to waive such notice.

To be valid such a notice must:

a be in writing.
b be given not less than four weeks before the end date it mentions.

The above requirements cannot be altered or waived by a tenancy agreement.

The following rules apply unless the agreement states otherwise.

The notice must:

a terminate the tenancy at the end of a complete period of tenancy (e.g. the end of a month, if the tenancy is by the month).

b be longer than four weeks if the period of tenancy is longer than four weeks.

Protection against harassment

It is a criminal offence for anyone unlawfully to turn a residential occupier out of his or her home or use threats, physical aggression, the witholding of services, or any other interference to try to drive him or her out. The local authority has power to prosecute such offenders.

Living conditions

If the dwelling is shared by more than one household, the landlord can be ordered by the local authority to bring it up to certain standards of cleanliness and soundness. Different authorities use these powers in different ways.

Unless the tenancy was signed before 24 October 1961 or is for more than seven years, the landlord is legally responsible for keeping the structure and exterior of the dwelling in good repair. He or she is also responsible by law for keeping basins, sinks, baths, and any other sanitary installations in good working order. The same legal obligations apply to installations for the supply of water, gas, electricity, and space heating.

Help towards rent and rates

It may be possible for the following types of young tenant to obtain rent and/ or rate relief:

people living in hostels
people earning less than the industrial average wage
people on low earnings with dependents
people in receipt of Social Security payments
council tenants
people who live in part of a commercial property (e.g. a flat above a shop)
people with certain disability pensions
one-parent families

This list is not exhaustive and it is always worth investigating possibilities for young people. Information on rates can be obtained from the local Council. Information on rents can be obtained from the local Rent Tribunal Office.

Anyone, regardless of age, who has contracted to pay rent can be sued for failing to do so.

What responsibilities do local authorities have?

The local authority has the power, but not the duty, to provide accommodation for young people.

The Housing (Homeless Persons) Act 1979 does make local authorities legally responsible for finding accommodation for young people who are unintentionally homeless and threatened with violence or exploitation.

The same Act compels local authorities to find accommodation, regardless of age, for anyone who is:

pregnant (or who already has children)
the victim of a home destroyed or badly damaged by accident including fire and flood
handicapped

When can young people legally leave home?

Legally young people can leave home when they like but parents and authorities can make a person under 18 the subject of a care order if it is felt that he or she is in moral danger or in need of care and control.

At 18 years of age a person has the right to determine where he or she lives.

Abduction

The laws of abduction centre around the forcing or enticing of young people to leave home. They apply in the following broad instances:

1. It is a criminal offence to force, trick, or entice a person under 14 years to leave home.
2. It is an offence similarly to persuade a girl under 16 years of age to leave home contrary to her parents wishes.
3. It is an offence to persuade a girl of 18 or younger to leave home against her wishes if it is by someone who intends to have unlawful sexual intercourse with her.

5 Legal procedures in Scotland

There are considerable differences between the laws in Scotland and those of England and Wales. Some of the main differences, relevant to the care of children and young adults, are summarized below.

Dealing with juveniles in criminal proceedings

In Scotland the age of criminal responsibility is eight. Children are not tried in juvenile courts but referred to **reporters** who are appointed by regional district authorities. They are trained in legal and/or social work and have the job of assessing what action should be taken. There are three main choices:

1 Take no action. This may be accompanied by the reporter warning parents that further misbehaviour will result in referral to a children's hearing.
2 Refer the case to the social work department of a local authority. This is only possible with the agreement of the parents who must be willing for the child to be supervised by the department.
3 Refer the case to a children's hearing.

Children's hearings

Children's panels are appointed by the Secretary of State to provide tribunals for children's hearings. They are made up of lay people from a cross-section of the community. The tribunals before whom young people appear are made up of three members of the children's panel including at least one man and one woman.

These hearings are not open to the public. The press may attend but may not publish details of the case. Normally the only persons present will be the child, his or her parents, the reporter (or his or her representative), and a social worker. The parents will be asked by the tribunal if they understand and accept the grounds for referral to the children's hearing. If there are disputes over the grounds the case will be referred to the Sheriff's court (see below) which will decide whether the grounds are valid. If they are, the case will be referred back.

The tribunal will conduct the hearing more informally than an English or Welsh juvenile court and discuss with those present what should be done. If it is decided not to dismiss the case, a 'supervision requirement' will be imposed. This requires the child to be supervised either in a named residential establishment (usually a borstal or detention centre) or at home under a social worker. An appeal against sentence can be lodged with the Sheriff's court. Reviews can be ordered at any time by the social work department and every three months by the parents.

Dealing with adults in criminal proceedings

The police do not prosecute in Scotland. All prosecution is brought by public prosecutors. There are two basic legal procedures in Scottish law: 'Summary Procedure' and 'Solemn Procedure'.

Under **Summary Procedure** cases are heard by a judge sitting without a jury.

Under **Solemn Procedure** cases are heard by a judge sitting with a jury of fifteen people.

Courts

There are four types of court in Scotland:

1 The **Court of Criminal Appeal** has the final court appeal functions of the House of Lords in England and Wales.

2 The **High Court of Justiciary** tries serious cases. Murder and rape and some other cases can only be heard in this court. The judge always sits with a jury in this court and may impose life sentences and unlimited fines. The prosecution is brought by public prosecutors called Advocates-depute.

3 The **Sheriff's Courts** are presided over by a Sheriff who may sit alone or with a jury. In this court cases are heard which are deemed by the public prosecutor—the Procurator Fiscal—to be sufficiently serious to be tried by a sheriff but not necessarily serious enough to go to the High Court. If the Sheriff sits alone the maximum sentences are three months' imprisonment or £1000 fine. If the Sheriff sits with a jury the maximum sentences are two years' imprisonment or an unlimited fine. The Sheriff may refer a case to the High Court for more severe sentence.

4 **District Courts** deal with minor offences including road traffic offences. They are presided over by Justices of the Peace who are not legally qualified but may be accompanied by Stipendiary Magistrates who are legally qualified and have the same powers as a Sheriff. Prosecution is brought by the Procurator Fiscal. The normal maximum sentences are 60 days' imprisonment or a £200 fine.

Sentences

There are no conditional discharges, suspended sentences, or sentences binding people over to keep the peace in Scottish Law. The following range of sentences are available to Scottish Courts:

1 **Absolute discharge** Effectively the same as in England and Wales but in Summary Proceedings it can be used without proceeding to conviction.

2 **Admonition** This involves an official reprimand but carries no obligations.

3 **Fine** This is dealt with in a similar way to the English and Welsh system.

4 **Probation** Similar to the English and Welsh system but not identical. In Summary Procedure it is possible for probation to be ordered without proceeding to conviction.

5 **Imprisonment** Similar to the English and Welsh system.

6 **Deferred sentence** The courts may defer sentence for a given period of time, after which if behaviour has been satisfactory they will usually fine or admonish. At the end of the given period they have the full sentencing powers which would have applied at the time of trial.

7 **Care and Custody of children** Children are protected by the Guardianship Act in Scotland, England, and Wales. With some minor variations of detail the general principles of law relating to the care and custody of children are the same in Scotland as they are in England and Wales.

Section E

Creating a caring institution

The caring environment

It is no good having an elaborate pastoral care system in an otherwise oppressive school or youth group. The larger the institution, the more difficult it is to keep a humane perspective on the way in which it is run. Nevertheless this perspective is precisely what is required.

This book has attempted to give a measure of support and guidance to those who have pastoral responsibility for young people. It was not, however, intended to give the impression that caring for people in an institution is a specialist function. All members of a school, college, or youth group have some responsibility for the well-being of all other members, whatever their status. This section sets out some of the issues which need to be addressed if schools, colleges, and youth groups are to become caring communities. To put it another way—here are some considerations which will certainly reduce the anxieties which your own unit may be causing while you (as an individual) battle on trying to help young people.

Management

1 **Who makes the rules and with whose help?**

Are these rules, including the procedures laid down for staff, sensible? Are they relevant?
Is there any facility for reviewing and changing them?
If so: Who can participate in such a review?
Who can participate in changing the system?

In many institutions there is a proportion of the system which dates back to a set of needs which are no longer relevant. People tend to behave with more dignity and feel more secure in systems which can respond to change.

2 **Who enforces the rules?**

Does the unit encourage participation in management?
Can people be heard if they have a grievance, with the assurance that their views will be respected?

There will always be unpleasant compromises to be made by individuals in any organization, but if people simply feel at the mercy of a preconceived management structure they will suffer quite unnecessary stress and learn little about responsibility.

3 **Is your institution clear about its referral points?**
In other words, who is responsible when various things go wrong or decisions need to be made?
Is there someone to check that communication and referral are working properly?
Is responsibility shared reasonably throughout the unit?

Lack of clarity about responsibility causes stress among staff and students alike. There is also the trap of certain people opting out while their more diligent colleagues martyr themselves with quite hopeless work-loads.

4 **Is the ability to understand and care for people a quality which is valued in the selection of new staff?**
Is there any facility for improving the interpersonal skills of staff once they are in post?

Teaching ability or leadership skills are often felt to be so important for those working with young people that it does not occur to anyone until it is too late that the person selected at interview is unable to cope with young people as people.

Curriculum

It isn't just schools and colleges which have a curriculum. All youth groups have a curriculum. In fact they have two—the overt one which appears on timetables and programmes; and the covert one which includes teaching approaches and the aims and ethos of the institution.

The overt curriculum

Does the curriculum give the impression that life is divided into separate compartments? In the process of enabling young people to acquire accreditation (exams, certificates, awards), does the curriculum seem to suggest that personal development and social skills are less important than the certificated skills? Is everyone so busy delivering the timetabled subjects that there is no possibility of responding to the students as people?

Deep water this, but we have been looking at anxiety, school-refusing, teenage pregnancy, and health problems. Are we so busy with the overt curriculum that we just miss the major life-events that are happening to young people? To what extent did we think that a slot on the timetable called health education or personal guidance was all we needed to ensure that people were able to cope? Do we only find out about young people when they present us with a problem?

The covert curriculum (teaching approaches)

1 Does your style enable people to communicate with you in a creative and dignified manner?
Are you interested in the young people with whom you work?
Do you use teaching approaches which encourage participation and self-expression?

Try listing your teaching methods or leadership approaches. If they allow people to contribute not only their ideas but their feelings, you will not be caught out when those people are in difficulties. You will have really participated in their emotional development and probably helped prevent some of the problems young people experience through feelings of isolation, inadequacy, and sheer frustration.

2 What sanctions and threats do you and your colleagues use? Are they deliberately, or inadvertently, degrading?
Do you tend to blame rather than understand?
Do you try to see the behaviour of young people in the widest possible context as well as in relation to the institutional framework?
Do you have the patience and confidence to allow time for things to impact on people so that they grow and change?

We cause problems whenever we diminish people. It is always because of our own uncertainty. We are afraid of things getting out of hand so we get the retaliation in first. Often we are having much more influence than we suspect. People need time and space to reconsider their behaviour and reform. There needn't be very many emergency disciplinary situations—but it is easy to get into a style of supervision which treats all situations like emergencies.

The covert curriculum (ethos and aims)

1 What are the stated values and aims of your institution?
What are the hidden values and aims?

Do you agree with them?

You need to know what the aims and values of your institution are and if you don't agree with them you need to decide what you are going to do to change them.

2 You will have seen that *On The Spot* places a high value on environments and relationships which:
- encourage people to take responsibility for their own actions;
- make people feel worthwhile both as individuals and as contributors to groups and the institution;
- give people the space to grow and change;
- encourage people to be understanding and helpful in their dealings with others;
- allow people to question their situation and confront issues;
- respect confidentiality;
- avoid stereotyping;
- don't take themselves too seriously.

3 A caring institution also places a high value on systems which:
- can look at themselves honestly and change if necessary;
- promote cooperative enterprise and shared goals;
- allow differences of opinion or conflicts of interest to be openly explored;
- are led by people who model the good behaviour they expect and avoid hypocrisy;
- are not isolationist but welcome influences from the community at large or other professional groups.

Support for you

A caring institution cares for all its members: what about you? Perhaps you bought this book because you tend to focus on other people's needs and wanted to be more helpful. Perhaps you bought it because you have been thrust into a pastoral role. Either way you will only really succeed if you yourself are cared for and can count on someone for personal support.

There are three kinds of personal support which are particularly important for those who have a caring role in an institution. Firstly, there should be someone, or a group of people, with whom you can discuss difficulties arising from your pastoral work and review tactics. A caring institution will ensure that such groups exist and allocate time for meetings of this kind. In such a support group it should be possible to identify areas of skill which members need to develop.

The second kind of personal support you need is opportunities for training. Interpersonal skills need constantly to be augmented and refreshed. Knowledge of particular problem areas and the resources available to deal with them also need updating.

Finally, you need and deserve someone who will help you with your own stresses and worries. You need this support because we all have emotional difficulties and need to deal with them before they become too dominant in our lives. You also need it because if you are frequently dealing with other people's distress, this can get linked to your own distress after a while, and you will find that your attention for others is not as good as it should be. Some institutions make sure the people who have a pastoral role have a personal supervisor. Ideally such a supervisor will not be a member of the institution. It needs to be someone who can offer you the kind of attention outlined in the counselling section of this book. To make the best use of such a person you need to make regular appointments to meet. Don't wait until things build up. If your supervisor is prepared to be on short-notice stand-by, so much the better. Find someone you trust and who is strong enough, and intelligent enough, not to be shocked or intimidated by any strong feelings you may want to bring out into the open. It also needs to be someone who can help you plan how you are going to deal with the inevitable emotional difficulties which are part of the job of caring for people. You owe it to the young people in your care to arrange the support you need so that you can concentrate on **them** when they come to you for help, and not on your own problems.

Useful agencies

1 British Association for Counselling

37A Sheep Street, Rugby, CV21 3BX *Tel:* 0788 78328/9

Purposes

BAC is the principal umbrella organization for all types of counselling and counsellors. Its aims are:

1 To promote understanding and awareness of counselling throughout society.
2 To increase the availability of counselling by trained and supervised counsellors.
3 To maintain and raise standards of counselling training and practice.
4 To provide support for counsellors and opportunities for their personal growth, education, and training.
5 To respond to the increasing demand for information and advice concerning both counselling and counsellors.
6 To represent counselling at national level.

Services

BAC runs an information service during office hours at its headquarters in Rugby. It offers a consultancy service, organizes conferences, and negotiates with government departments and charities to promote counselling in many different settings.

The Audio-Visual Aids Unit hires out films and videos and runs viewing days and workshops on the use of audio-visual material in counselling training.

The Association runs an accreditation scheme to maintain standards of counselling and publishes a code of ethics (acceptance of which is a condition of membership) to protect client and counsellor alike.

Structure

BAC is a charity which derives its funding from subscriptions, donations, and grant aid from independent bodies.

The Association is organized into six divisions specializing in specific areas of counselling:

The Association for Pastoral Care and Counselling (APCC)

The Association for Student Counselling (ASC)
Counselling at Work (CAW)
Counselling in Education (CIE)
Counselling in Medical Settings (CMS)
Personal, Sexual, Marital, Family Division (PSMF)

Members, who may be individuals or organizations, may belong to more than one division. There are also branches organized on a regional basis.

Publications

The quarterly journal *Counselling* and the newsletter are sent free to members. BAC also publishes a range of short books and pamphlets on aspects of counselling. Another series concentrates on areas of need such as redundancy, physical disablement, and bereavement. The Association publishes a number of directories of use to counsellors and/or clients which cover such topics as referral, training, and psychosexual counselling.

2 The National Youth Bureau

17–23 Albion Street, Leicester LE1 6GD *Tel:* 0533 554775

Founded in 1973, the Bureau is the national resource centre for workers involved in the social education of young people (youthworkers, teachers, social workers, careers officers, etc.) and provides information, publications, and joint action on youth affairs.

Structure

The Bureau is a registered charity and is governed by a council of the principal bodies involved in youth affairs (local authority associations, professional bodies, voluntary organizations).

Funding is mainly from central government sources, DES, DHSS, Home Office, and MSC. Some funding is derived from trusts and industry.

The Bureau has a staff of seventy under a Director and Heads of Units. At the time of publishing this book, the Bureau's management was under review by the government and some changes expected.

Services

The Bureau acts as a national clearing house and library for publications and texts connected with the social education of young people. It is open, by appointment, to visitors for the inspection of this material and will also loan documents. In addition to supplying advice and resource materials for training, the Bureau will offer staff support for the mounting of conferences and workshops.

The Bureau acts as a locus and support centre for five developmental units:

1 Youth Counselling Development Unit (YCDU). (See NAYPCAS p. 116.)

2 Youth Social Work Unit (YSWU) Funded by the DHSS it focuses on young people at risk or in trouble. (See also intermediate treatment pp. 90–1.)
3 Youth Opportunities Development Unit (YODU) Funded by MSC, it provides an information and advisory service on the transition from school to work.
4 Youth Work Unit (YWU) Funded by the DES to offer information, training, and development services to full and part-time youthworkers.
5 Young Volunteer Resources Unit (YVRU) Funded by the Voluntary Services Unit of the Home Office to provide training, support, information, and developmental services to those concerned with community involvement by young people.

The Bureau acts as the employer for staff for the In-Service Training and Education Panel (INSTEP) which coordinates and endorses in-service training programmes for full-time youth and community workers.

The Bureau provides accommodation for the National Council for Voluntary Youth Services (NCVYS).

Publications

The Bureau publishes two monthly magazines, *Youth in Society* and *Scene*.

Youth in Society is a well-presented glossy journal which features articles and reviews by leading writers in the field of social education. It also incorporates a digest of recent publications and training materials.

Scene is a newspaper-style publication which is aimed more specifically at the part-time youthworker. It takes a lively look at current political and social issues affecting the lives and prospects of young people.

The Bureau offers a range of reference books, reports, surveys, training packs, incidental papers, and reprints of standard texts which have been deleted by publishers.

3 NAYPCAS—National Association of Young People's Counselling and Advisory Services

Based at the National Youth Bureau (Youth Counselling Development Unit), 17–23 Albion Street, Leicester, LE1 6GD *Tel:* 0533 554775

Purposes

This is the umbrella organization for youth counselling and advisory services, whether voluntary or professional. It exists to promote, develop, and support such agencies. It provides a forum for the exchange of ideas and good practice. It is also active in promoting public and political recognition for the need for these services.

Services

NAYPCAS runs an information service during office hours at its headquarters. It offers consultancy teams who will visit agencies or link with individuals. It runs national training workshops for counsellors and advisory workers using the leading trainers in various relevant fields.

Structure
Members are predominately part-time volunteers but there are, of course, a substantial number of professionals: either full-time agency directors or youthworkers, school counsellors, social workers, etc. It is from this wide body of members that most of the resource for providing consultancy and training is derived, but a full-time secretary and two full-time development officers are based in Leicester.

Publications
NAYPCAS Newsfront (quarterly or in response to particular current events). The *Newsfront* comes in a mailing package which will often include such things as reading and conference lists, extracts from recent government acts or surveys, and guidelines on difficult aspects of counselling.

4 NSPCC—National Society for the Prevention of Cruelty to Children

1 Riding House Street, London, W1P 8AA *Tel:* 01 580 8812

Purposes
This society exists to prevent child abuse in all its forms; to give practical help to families in which the children are at risk; to raise public consciousness of the nature and causes of child abuse; and to promote and sponsor research into new methods of tackling the problems.

Services
In support of the above objects the society offers a round-the-clock service to children and families in need. Through this service over 50 000 children are helped each year. At its headquarters the society maintains a specialist library and consultancy service. A national network of drop-in centres and therapeutic and community playgroups has been established. There is a youth section called the Young League of the NSPCC.

Structure
The work is spearheaded by 230 full-time inspectors who have statutory powers to initiate care proceedings where appropriate (see pp. 101–2). In eleven local authorities joint funded special units have been established. The society recruits local volunteers.

Publications
Child's Guardian (twice yearly)
How the NSPCC works to protect children Annual review

5 The Manpower Services Commission (MSC)

Moorfoot, Sheffield S14PQ *Tel:* 0742 753275

Also contact through your Area Office as listed in local directory.

The Manpower Services Commission is a central government agency which was set up for two main purposes: firstly to extend and improve job-related training for adults and young people; secondly to create new employment opportunities.

The two arms of the MSC with most relevance to educators are the Training Division and the Technical and Vocational Education Initiative Board.

Training Division Amongst other duties, this division administers the Youth Training Scheme for school-leavers under 18. The division is organized into Area Offices which serve local authority areas (sometimes in combinations of two or three). Each Area is administered by an Area Manager who is a Principal Civil Servant and served by a lay committee of employers, educators, union representatives, and careers officers, called an Area Manpower Board. This Board vets scheme proposals and advises on policy for MSC-sponsored training for the area it serves.

Technical and Vocational Education Initiative Board TVEI is a curriculum innovation programme aimed at improving and extending vocational education in schools. It provides funding and advice for selected schemes involving pupils in the 14–18 age range. Schemes usually operate within a cluster of schools linked to a college of further education.

Both the above schemes have had an enormous impact on education and are likely to continue to do so. As a publisher, MSC has been responsible for a number of manuals, guidelines, and discussion documents. These are generally of high quality, drawing on the expertise of respected researchers and curriculum designers. Some of the publications have been concerned with counselling and guidance which is a compulsory feature of both Youth Training Scheme courses and Technical and Vocational Education Initiative programmes.

6 Agencies concerned with counselling and the training of counsellors

Human Potential Research Project, Adult Education Department, University of Surrey, Guildford.

Provides training in a style of reciprocal peer group counselling developed by John Heron. This style of counselling is particularly suitable for the support and supervision sessions described briefly in the last section of this book. There are groups using and promoting this type of counselling throughout Britain and the above Project may be able to supply local contact addresses on request.

The Tavistock Institute of Human Relations, 102 Belsize Lane, London NW3
For a number of years the Tavistock has been at the forefront of training in a wide variety of counselling and human growth methodologies. It is a leading agency for the promotion of all applications of humanistic psychology.

7 Agencies concerned with health and family planning

Brook Advisory Centres, 223 Tottenham Court Road, London W1P 9AE
Tel: 01 323 1522 *or* 01 580 2991
The centres provide free birth control advice and counselling on matters of sex and relationships for young people. They are staffed by doctors, nurses, and social workers. The central office and some of the sub-offices have a resource bank of learning materials related to sexuality and birth control. There are centres in Birmingham, Bristol, Cambridge, Coventry, Edinburgh, London and Liverpool.

Family Planning Association, 27–35 Mortimer Street, London W1N 7RJA
Tel: 01 636 7866
The Association pioneered family planning clinical services in this country but handed these over to the NHS in 1974–6. It now provides information and education on family planning and sexual problems. The FPA Information Service has a very wide range of health care leaflets, videos, and films which are available for educators. The Association runs training for all types of educators and health care workers throughout the UK.

8 Agencies concerned with support and information for parents

British Agencies for Adoption and Fostering, 11 Southwark Street, London SE1 1RQ
Seeks to inform the public about the social, medical, and psychological issues related to adoption and fostering. Also seeks to promote good practice. Provides training conferences and written information services. Journal: *Adoption and Fostering* (quarterly)

National Marriage Guidance Council (HQ), Herbert Gray College, Little Church Street, Rugby, Warwicks CV21 3AP *Tel:* 0788 73241
There are about 150 Marriage Guidance Councils throughout England, Wales, and N. Ireland providing counselling for problems related to marriage and family life. The college above runs a mail-order book service.

Organization for Parents Under Stress, 29 Newmarket Way, Hornchurch, Essex RM12 6DR *Tel:* 04024 51538
Set up to prevent child abuse and maltreatment of infants and young children by providing a network of self-help groups for parents under stress. Runs a befriending service, telephone helplines, and drop-in centres.

Professional back-up for local initiatives is available.

Parents Anonymous, 6–9 Manor Gardens, London N7 6LA *Tel:* 01 669 8900 (6p.m.–6a.m.)
Offers friendship and help to child abusers or would-be child abusers. Aims to improve the public understanding of the needs to such families. Runs an information service, telephone counselling by trained volunteers, and a national network of self-help groups.

9 Agencies of general interest to educators

Child Poverty Action Group, 1 Macklin Street, London WC2B JNH
Tel: 01 242 3225 *or* 01 242 9149
Set up for the direct and indirect relief of families affected by poverty. This organization is now a major voice for policies on this matter. It offers research, information, and conferences. Journal: *Poverty*.

National Association of Youth Clubs, 70 St. Nicholas Circle, Leicester LE1 JNY *Tel:* 0533 29514
Apart from acting as a general resource unit for youth clubs, this organization has sponsored special projects in such things as detached youthwork, homelessness, community industry, intermediate treatment and political education. It has a variety of informational leaflets and films and various publications.

National Children's Bureau, 8 Wakley Street, Islington, London EC1V 7QE *Tel:* 01 278 9441
Amongst general aims concerned with the development of children the Bureau acts as a catalyst to bring together educational, medical, and social work agencies to promote the well-being of children. Runs conferences, training and an information service. Journal: *Concern* (quarterly).

NOISE (National Organization for Initiatives in Social Education), Bayswater Centre, 15 Bayswater Avenue, Bristol BS6 7NU
Promotes links between alternative social education centres, mainstream education, and other relevant agencies. Provides a forum for an exchange of ideas and expertise amongst those concerned with social education provision in and out of school. Seeks to influence the formulation of both national and local authority policy with respect to the education of disaffected young people. Publishes *NOISE*—a termly journal, and arranges conferences, workshops, information services, and consultancy.

The Careers Research and Advisory Centre (CRAC), Bateman Street, Cambridge, CB2 1LZ *Tel:* 0223 354551
CRAC exists to provide links between education and employment and to improve careers counselling and guidance.

CRAC runs courses and conferences for teachers, lecturers, industrialists, students, and young managers. CRAC provides an advisory service for educators involved in careers education and business education.

CRAC publishes books and guides on educational and employment opportunities and resource materials for job-related courses. It also sponsors projects and smaller units.

The National Institute for Careers Education and Counselling (NICEC), The Hatfield Polytechnic, Bayfordbury House, Lower Hatfield Road, Hertford SE13 8LD

NICEC is sponsored jointly by CRAC (see above) and Hatfield Polytechnic. It exists to advance the development of careers education and counselling services.

NICEC provides training and staff development courses for educators with counselling and guidance responsibilities. It also runs an advisory service for teachers, FE lecturers and Youth Training Scheme instructors.

The NICEC research unit supplies data on the careers guidance processes and techniques to support the training carried out by CRAC (see above.)

Further reading

1 Counselling

General Introductions to counselling

AXLINE V. *Dibs in Search of Self* Pelican (1964)
An account of the relationship between a pioneering child psychiatrist and a severely disturbed child. Witty, moving, and enjoyable, it yields valuable insights into emotional growth and the therapeutic relationship. Although it describes a long-term psychiatric process it does so in such a way as to be extremely relevant to the lay counsellor and is rightly included on most counselling reading lists.

EGAN G. *The Skilled Helper* Brooks Cole (1975)
A skills approach to counselling which offers a useful introduction. Takes the reader through counselling processes step by step and includes clear descriptions of a range of techniques.

KENNEDY E. *On Becoming a Counsellor* Gill and Macmillan (1977)
A well-tried introductory text. Straightforward and readable. Good description of the counselling relationship and details of various basic techniques.

PROCTOR B. *Counselling Shop* André Deutsch (1978)
Gives a taste of some of the main current counselling approaches through interviews with their leading exponents. A good way of surveying the field and perhaps choosing a type of counselling to pursue through training.

2 Pastoral care and the counselling of adolescents and young adults

HAMBLIN D. *The Teacher and Pastoral Care* Basil Blackwell (1978)
Sound approach to a variety of challenges facing teachers. Good on dealing with aggression.

HAMBLIN D. *Guidance 16–19* Basil Blackwell (1983)
Practical guide to involving young adults in the task of guidance and pastoral care. Summarizes the points made in tables and provides a framework for pastoral groupwork.

JONES A. *Counselling Adolescents in School* Kogan Page (1977)
Suggests ways of establishing a counselling service in school and explains basic counselling techniques. Very good section on the difficult questions and statements which reveal the major concerns of young people. Useful case studies.

McGUINESS J.B. *Planned Pastoral Care* McGraw-Hill (1982)
Not recommended as an introduction but raises some important points about school issues such as pupil records, assessment, and referral.

McMASTER J.M. (ed.) *Methods in Social and Educational Caring* Gower Press (1982)
Aimed at community-based workers as well as teachers. Describes pastoral groupwork in action. Good description of some methods of behaviour modification and a sound critique of intermediate treatment.

McMASTER J.M. (ed.) *Skills in Social and Educational Caring* Gower Press (1982)
Useful discussions of counselling in educational settings, the training of counsellors and groupworkers, and the skills required in supervision. A bit technical at times but practical and thorough.

MARLAND M. *Pastoral Care* Heinemann Educational Books (1979)
Tackles the difficult subject of school pastoral organization and the roles of teachers. Good on the involvement of parents.

MILLER J.C. *The Guidance and Counselling Role of the Tutor in Vocational Preparation* FEU (Further Education Curriculum Review and Development Unit) (1983)
One of the few good texts on counselling which concentrates on the Further Education context. Highly recommended as an introduction to counselling not only for FE tutors but YTS trainers and teachers in sixth forms.

MUCCHIELLI R. *Face to Face in the Counselling Interview* Macmillan (1984)
Deals with theory and practice in two complete texts printed so that you can begin with either in the same book. Very clear on both subjects. The practice text has exercises with write-in columns for the reader's notes. A good source of definitions, theories, examples, and approaches. Accessible to anyone.

NOONAN E. *Counselling Young People* Methuen (1983)
This is for people who want to tackle in-depth counselling and contains sections on diagnosis which go further than many counsellors would recommend. On the other hand it has useful sections on authority and responsibility, and the organization of counselling.

MURGATROYD D. *Helping the Troubled Child—Interprofessional Case Studies* Harper & Row (1980)
The case studies do indeed clarify procedure, roles, and problems of referral. A good text for preparing educationalists for extending their sense of colleagueship and re-defining responsibilities.

RUTTER M. *Helping Troubled Children* Penguin (1975)
On the borderline between a medical and lay approach to helping. Provides a framework for determining the seriousness of problems and is clear about the priorities for helpers. A comprehensive account of the cases and manifestations of problem areas.

TURNER C. *Developing Interpersonal Skills* Further Education Staff College, Soombe Lodge (1983)
A good introduction to humanistic psychology and some of its applications in counselling and educational management. The examples are in the FE context but relevant throughout education. Provides excellent descriptions of transactional analysis and assertiveness training. Shows how to apply interpersonal skills in interviews, groups, meetings, assessment, and management. Highly recommended.

3 Helping the disrupter

GALLOWAY, BALL, BLOMFIELD, AND SEYD *Schools and Disruptive Pupils* Longman (1982)
A survey of Sheffield's attempts to deal with disruptive students. Useful mainly for the way it explores the effects of school organization on the incidence of disruption. Also some good details on how withdrawal units are run.

TOPPING K. *Educational Systems for Disruptive Adolescents* Croom/Helm (1983)
Looks at a wide range of tactics from off-site units to para-professional staff. Not focused primarily on relationships and full of references and technical terms. On the other hand it is a useful way of surveying what has become a specialist field.

4 Adolescence

ODLUM D. *Adolescence* Wayland Press (1983)
Non-technical account of the main problems encountered by young people during adolescence. Aimed at parents and teachers but useful for anyone, including adolescents.

5 Sexuality and Sexual Problems

BANCROFT J. (ed.) *Human Sexuality and its Problems* Churchill Livingstone (1983)
Although tackling the whole range of human sexuality this book contains some of the best discussions about young people in contemporary society.

CHEETHAM J. *Unwanted Pregnancy and Counselling* Routledge Kegan Paul (1978)
Tackles a comprehensive analysis of the psychological and social background to unwanted pregnancy as well as 'Ways of Helping' and 'Aspects of Counselling'. Very readable basic text for anyone who may become involved with helping pregnant girls and young women.

FARRELL C. *My Mother Said...* Routledge Kegan Paul (1978)
If you don't believe there are communication problems about sex, read this! Contains accounts of how young people learn about sex—and what they learn, and what they don't!

Pregnant at School
A survey published by the National Council for One-Parent Families and the Community Development Trust. A thorough and revealing study of the incidence and some of the effects of early sexuality and precocious motherhood. An important document for educators.

A Place to Go (Video)
Obtainable from the Department of Medical Illustration, John Radcliffe Hospital. Good straightforward depiction of a Young People's Advisory Clinic in action. Shows good investigative counselling and practical advice.

The Family Planning Association, 27–35 Mortimer Street, London W1 issues a wide range of free leaflets, booklets, and posters on birth control and all aspects of sexual relationships.

6 The Law

The following give a useful outline of legislation and legal procedures affecting young people.

PACE P. J. *Family Law* M & E Handbooks (1981)

PRIOR C. *Rights, Responsibilities and the Law—Introduction for Teachers* Cobden Trust (1983)

SMITH R. *Children and the Courts* Sweet & Maxwell (1979)

Index